*Ties That Blind in
Canadian/American Relations:
Politics of News Discourse*

COMMUNICATION

A series of volumes edited by:
Dolf Zillmann and **Jennings Bryant**

Ties That Blind in
Canadian/American Relations:
Politics of News Discourse

Richard L. Barton
The Pennsylvania State University

 LAWRENCE ERLBAUM ASSOCIATES, PUBLISHERS
1990   Hillsdale, New Jersey   Hove and London

Lawrence Erlbaum Associates, Inc., Publishers
365 Broadway
Hillsdale, New Jersey 07642

Library of Congress Cataloging-in-Publication Data

Barton, Richard L.
    Ties That Blind in Canadian/
  American relations: Politics
  of News Discourse/Richard L. Barton.
        p. cm. — (Communication)
    Includes bibliographical references.
    ISBM 0-8058-0743-8
    1. United States — Relations — Canada. 2. Canada — Relations — United
  States. 3. Journalism — Political aspects — United States.
  4. Journalism — Political aspects — Canada. 5. Foreign news — United
  States. I. Title. II. Series: Communication (Hillsdale, N.J.)
  E183.8C2B35   1990
  303.48'273071 — dc20

Printed in United States of America
10 9 8 7 6 5 4 3 2 1

To Dick, Helen, Mud, and Ann

Contents

Preface

This book explores the political impact of journalistic discourse on international relations. Its main points, examples, and arguments are based on a comparative analysis of American and international press accounts of selected issues in Canadian/American relations. Although the intention of the book is to enhance our understanding of the political significance of journalists' interpretations of Canadian/American relations as a specific case of international politics, the communication perspective and method of news analysis of the book are appropriate for the study of the United States' news-mediated relations with other countries as well. This study also concerns itself with the way people negotiate news-mediated political discourse and how that communication process has the potential to influence international affairs.

The book is divided into two major sections; a theoretical framework is proposed and serves as the basis for the method of analyzing international news. The remainder of the book applies this method specifically to news about Canadian/American affairs.

Several assumptions about the nature of news-mediated political communications shape the book's process of inquiry. Among them is the belief that news reports about international affairs constitute a distinctive form of political discourse that has implications for the relations among nations. Both the successes and failures in America's history of dealing with Canada are, in large part, attributable to political communication processes that involve journalistic discourse.

The variety of political visions brought to international news discourse influences Canadian/American relations in profound ways. The participants in this discourse include news reporters, news organizations, citizens, bureaucrats, lobbyists, and policymakers.

The news about Canadian/American affairs is but one of many interactive symbolic opportunities that form the larger communication context for the players who might influence Canadian/American relations. The political vision of these players in the drama of mass-mediated relations is resistant to, "blind" to interpretations that confront, deviate from the "reality" of the political cultures with which they are most closely associated. People shape and interpret news texts about Canadian/American relations on the basis of their attachment to and movement through these cultures. Even individuals and groups who, on the surface, appear to be apolitical participate in public discourse in politically significant ways. For example, *not* tuning in to television news has political implications. Opting out of this form of public discourse about American foreign policy might lead one to use alternative press sources. And those who use news accounts in passive, uncritical ways, making no attempt to influence the opinion and political behavior of their peers, tend to reinforce existing policies. Similarly, the extent to which individuals "read" the news with varying degrees of knowledge about the history of Canadian/American relations reflects politically significant communication patterns that confront or accept journalists' definitions of policies and processes in international relations.

There is a popular assumption, in western democracies, that the norm of journalistic objectivity guides responsible journalism. Presumptions about the inherent persuasive potential of certain news forms (such as television's apparently objective display of "real-life, as-it-happens" visuals) require that we attempt to understand journalism's many forms *comparatively* as they perform their roles in the complex discourse among the players in the drama of international relations. Journalism not only shares many of the characteristic "ties" that blind international political discourse in general, but contributes some additional ties of its own through specialized communication practices. One of the ironies of the involvement of news reports in international political discourse is that, contrary to the presumed pluralistic function of journalism in western democracies, news language frequently inhibits rather than facilitates positive international relations.

American characterizations of the "shared culture" of North America are typically broadly cast; Canadian/American relations are described as "that special relationship." More frequently, Canada is generically represented as "our steadfast, friendly neighbor to the north." One only has to recall the differences in the ideological roots of the two countries (America actively embraced and celebrated its revolutionary character, whereas Canada earnestly sought to build a conservative society, distinctively *independent* from America's) to question the adequacy of most American representations of Canada's political culture. International political analysts are preoccupied with the recent decline of America's international power. As

Canada becomes increasingly active as an international force, bringing to the international forum a tradition of diplomacy, intentions to be a key player in world trade, a culture steeped in multiculturalism, and a citizenry aggressively committed to the natural environment, it seems appropriate to investigate how American news informs us about the Canadian culture, Canadian politics, the Canadian/American alliance, and how that reportage might influence the dynamics of international affairs.

ACKNOWLEDGMENTS

I am indebted to friends and colleagues who have assisted in this project. Sandy Rawlins established a tradition of precise and creative archival assistance in helping me work through the volumes of international news material during the early stages of this research. The tradition was sustained by her successors in that job, Joe Gow and Serra Tinic. Bonnie Schaedel's patience, efficiency, and helpful suggestions while typing the final manuscript are appreciated. Dennis Gouran reviewed early drafts of the manuscript and provided a full measure of support throughout the project. Milo Pekarek's enthusiasm and sustained interest in the book were inspiring and contributed greatly to its completion.

Research support from the Canadian Embassy, Washington, DC, for several previous studies that served as the foundation for this book is gratefully acknowledged.

Finally, thanks to John R. Shepherd for introducing me to an "alternative" view of Canadian culture, and for suggesting that we Americans might have something to learn from the Canadians.

Richard L. Barton

Introduction

Perhaps it is a universal truth that the loss of liberty at home is to be charged
to provisions against danger, real or pretended, from abroad
— James Madison[1]

Columnist Russell Baker, apparently frustrated by the tendency of news
selectively to overdramatize world events, concluded that "today all the
world's a stage, the public's only an audience, and the journalist is like the
guy who used to stand outside the tents working his mouth to draw a
crowd" (p. A31).[2] This book investigates how the American press is
"working its mouth" about Canada's role in international affairs and what,
if anything, that news coverage has to do with what is going on inside the
"tent" of Canadian/American relations. Of special concern here is the way
the news "draws" the "crowd" by the use of its particular kind of language
and the appeals inherent in that language.

As its general theme, this book suggests that when American journalism
organizes its coverage of Canadian affairs within the context of ongoing
international press coverage, a more refined and responsive public discourse
about Canadian/American affairs is likely to be encouraged. As a result,
the enriched discourse, especially among politically active news consumers,
will make positive contributions to improving the relations between these
two countries. But this suggestion is immediately confronted by current
assumptions about the nature of media influence in general and, more
specifically, about the nature and influence of the world press as propaganda. The ubiquitous term *propaganda* is an ill-defined and often misused
communications concept in international relations studies. It is too often

used as a catch-all term in attempts to describe complex communication processes that defy easy explanations. A brief sketch of some of the ways in which propaganda is assumed to play a role in public discourse about international affairs follows.

Language used by the American government under President Ronald Reagan demonstrated that particular administration's abiding belief that "winning public opinion" was essential to accomplishing America's foreign policy objectives. This view had America "propagandizing" its way through international relations, and assumed that the very act of propagandizing, as an organized international communications enterprise, has political significance. One assessment of the Reagan administration's propaganda strategy concluded that:

> Under President Reagan . . . the tone of American propaganda has become more aggressive and the machine has been extensively refurbished, though it should be said that as its run-down was caused by considerations other than those of effectiveness, so the same is true of its rejuvenation. Firstly, the new American emphasis on propaganda is consistent with President Reagan's background as a professional communicator. Secondly, it has enabled his administration to claim that it is *doing something [sic]* about the Russians. . . . (pp. 123–124)[3]

Meanwhile, the Reagan Administration tended to treat international communications *from* other nations ethnocentrically as if they were bizarre, propagandistic, and threatening to national security. Because there is a persistent tendency for government agencies to assume that information intended as propaganda will have that effect on those who use it, citizens are encouraged to believe that the control of those communications is best left in the hands of those to whom we entrust our military-security-intelligence activities.

Several years ago there was a U.S.–Soviet proposal to make U.S. and Soviet international short wave radio broadcasts more freely available to mass audiences in both countries. The agreement, an offshoot of the Reagan–Gorbachev talks in Iceland, was intended to foster cross-cultural understanding and thereby reduce tension between the two countries. The tension, from the Soviet point of view, was attributable to perceptions of the lack of reciprocity in broadcasts between the two cultures:

> Mr. Gorbachev said that during the Iceland meeting, he raised with Mr. Reagan "the unequal situation" of radio broadcasts beamed at each other's countries. He was referring to the fact that a large share of Soviet households have radio sets that have a wide range of frequencies, allowing them to hear western broadcasts beamed at the Soviet Union. In the United States, most radio sets are designed for domestic broadcasting in the medium-wave, or AM

range, and do not pick up short wave broadcasts from Moscow, for example. (p. A8)[4]

For his part, Gorbachev argued that the Soviets "jammed" (electronically blocked) Voice of America radio broadcasts because "the United States did not provide an equal opportunity for Soviet broadcasts to reach Americans" (p. A8).[5] The proposal has since faded from view. There was considerable opposition to the idea in the United States. To some, it was preposterous; why make Radio Moscow propaganda available to Americans? After all, they argued, both countries have a history of intentionally blocking and confusing the reception of these services by their citizens in the belief that such communications were harmful communications. In fact, there was real concern that some Americans would be "taken in" by the Soviet propaganda if the proposal were accepted. (The Soviets had proposed making Radio Moscow available on regular AM radio frequencies.) This mechanistic, stimulus–response notion of propaganda is further revealed in the American reaction to Soviet involvement in Intelsat. The Soviets have used Intelsat for years. In fact, the "Hot-Line" between Moscow and Washington uses an Intelsat link. But as the Soviets' desire to become a major force in the development and use of communications satellites edged closer to reality on the occasion of their meeting with the 109 nation national Telecommunications Satellite organization, United States Information Agency (USIA) analysts concluded:

> Intersputnik provides the Soviet Union with several political and propaganda advantages, which could be strengthened by the agreement with Intelsat. For example, Intersputnik coordinates radio and television news, as well as broader political information and cultural policies, among Warsaw Pact broadcasters and their allies. (p. D5)[6]

But these policies for dealing with international communications seem ill-founded in light of reasoned communication analysis. For the definitions and characteristics typically ascribed to Soviet news "propaganda," as one example, do not convincingly separate that discourse from domestic discourse.

> Communist propaganda techniques include selection and exclusion, overemphasis, underemphasis, repetition, campaigns, argumentation, emotionalism, diversion, indirection, satire, ridicule and mockery. (pp. 125–126)[7]

Frequently, propaganda is identified as an essential element in news. Merrill and Lowenstein observe that:

> In practice, many students of propaganda recognize that the very best propaganda vehicle is the so-called objective, neutral, dispassionate news report . . . propaganda is on every page of a newspaper, and on every radio or television news show. (p. 191)[8]

And recently, the Voice of America was labeled by one of its own journalists as a "news organization in the custody of a propaganda organization (the United States Information Agency)" (p. 43).[9]

The point of this discussion is that most definitions of propaganda reside in behavioral notions of "message impact" and deny that media use involves negotiated discourse. Even in those instances in which *domestic* propaganda is recognized as a force in international relations, propaganda appeals are seen as accomplishing very specific objectives. Here is a view in which people are "targets":

> In some particular instances, as the case of the American intervention in Grenada suggests, testimonials can bring attitude changes, particularly regarding policies or topics about which targets have little previous information or not set attitudes. (p. 212)[10]

The language of government agencies, academic researchers, and the American domestic press tends to invest international communication opportunities with notions of propaganda in ways that repress rather than invite participation in political discourse that is informed by a world view. This language reveals the tendency of cultures, whether governmental, academic, or politically active citizens, to exercise control over communications that they perceive as politically significant to their objectives.

The perspective of this book assumes that the meanings of a particular news message reside in the interaction of the form of the message, the political orientation of the person who attends to the message and his or her informed political judgment. This is also an appropriate perspective from which to assess the propagandistic potential of news. For it assumes that international news discourse, including its "propaganda messages," will be confronted by the judgment of people who attend to the news. In the process of negotiating this discourse, people will discover flaws of logic, contempt for historical fact, insufficient proofs, and the like just as they do when "reading" domestic news. Improved access to international journalism would allow us to "demystify" the dreaded propaganda machine. Propaganda would be revealed for what it is and accepted or rejected accordingly. The credibility of the news sources would suffer the consequences. For international news can be judged against other news sources, interpersonal and group communications, and politically "read" arts and cultural messages. To conclude otherwise is to put into question the ideal of open political participation in western democracies, and to suggest that individual political influence is a chimera, that citizens from a variety of backgrounds are incapable of this kind of critical reading of public discourse, and that critical judgment is a privileged communication attribute not generally available to those who want to influence policy. Although the practice of critical news reading might not be as routine as we would hope, that fact is more a reflection of our inability to teach and encourage those skills than of a tendency for a specific demographic group selectively to monopolize them. Those who are politically active do, in fact, forage through a range of mainstream, prestige, and subcultural alternative press material to inform themselves about policy. Some do so more than others, as the issues and their own mix of political cultures move them. The poorly researched international short wave listener is a case in point. Those who subscribe to internationally tuned political publications, whether arch conservative or flamingly liberal, are soon aware of the variety and energy of this universe of publishing, with its insistent postal barrage of messages entreating one to subscribe so as to be even more politically effective. Here is a recent proposition from the publishers of *World Monitor*. It accompanied an invitation to become a charter subscriber:

> You and I truly live in a global community. We're no longer simply affected by neighborhood events or news from City Hall. The goings-on in other cities and countries have a real and dramatic impact on the way we live our lives and plan our futures.
>
> Even seemingly unrelated events — such as the political stability of the economic growth of other countries — can influence the price of food on our dinner table.

The appeals are replete with intermedia competition; the shortcomings of mainstream news media are confronted.

> On a day to day basis, it's hard to know exactly what is going on. Listening to the news or reading the papers may give you a glimpse, but catchy headlines and 3-minute news segments don't really give you the story behind the story. They don't tell you the why's and wherefore's . . . the real, human stories of pain and frustration . . . the hopes and aspirations, that lurk behind the glamour of TV, radio and newspaper coverage.
>
> Today the global village we live in requires that we know more about the world around us than at any other time in history.[11]

For the most part, however, these are still "alternative" voices to the political discourse of the mainstream press. Mainstream American journalism shares a fundamentally dismissive attitude toward international affairs and the communications through which those relations are defined and maintained. Essentially, this study concerns itself with rhetorical forms that reveal the political judgments of journalists and the audience. Journalists' judgments determine the difference between disclosing information in the public forum or keeping it secret, safe from evaluative discourse. Central to these judgments are opportunities for inviting questions to be raised, making comparisons among political ideologies and for encouraging the practice of critical analysis of international affairs. Regardless of the motivation or intention behind those judgments, either decision shapes public discourse and the policies informed by it. Further, the pattern of disclosure reinforces the ways in which people align themselves to "those two sovereign antonymies, the public and the private" (p. 149).[12]

The pervasive and repetitive nature of news encourages us to suspect that there must be significant political implications in journalism's coverage of international affairs. This suspicion often leads to a sense of antagonism about the role of the news in the presentation of international affairs. For example, Canadians are concerned that American television news does not pay enough attention to things Canadian.[13]

Research dealing specifically with television's coverage of international affairs reveals that of the 50 most frequently mentioned nations in U.S. network TV coverage between 1972 and 1981, Canada tied with Switzerland for 19th place.[14] Perhaps U.S. television news, assuming that all is well, takes Canadian/American relations for granted. Some Canadian watchers might argue that it is in the nature of network news in this country to dwell on crisis and catastrophe and that the absence of news about Canada in a sense is a positive sign of the health of Canadian/American relations. But that view seems too simplistic when one considers the historical ties, the long-term significance of economic (Canada and the U.S. are the world's largest trading partners) and political relations between the two countries.

From a political communications perspective, the tendency for the research to draw conclusions about the implications of news coverage of Canada from quantitative measures alone is disturbing. We need to move beyond questions relating to the number of minutes, the comparative number of news story categories, number of column inches, and story length devoted to Canada. It might be more useful to ask questions about how meaning is made from news about Canada; about the contexts in which that occurs, and the political implications of that meaning. For example, how significant is the meaning imbedded in the coverage that does exist for Canadian/American relations? What images are projected in what context, and how might they be implicated in American's foreign policy as it relates to Canada? How do different news forms (e.g., newspaper, television, international broadcast news) compare in their representations of Canadian/American politics?

U.S. scholars dealing with news about international affairs have done little to try to understand how the news portrays the state of Canadian/American affairs. One of the key studies dealing with news coverage of international affairs concluded that "remarkably little" has been published about U.S. news coverage of Canada.[15]

Studies of news form and function in Canadian/American relations constitute, in their own right, a discursive tradition that has a particular focus. That focus is an inevitable reflection of the tensions that have characterized our history. The overriding preoccupation in the research is the extent to which American and Canadian news services present reportage that works against the development of Canada's cultural sovereignty and national identity. This research, based mainly on content analysis methods, includes studies of cross-border news flow, comparisons of Canadian and American news content, the "contamination" of Canadian perspectives by American media and studies of the potential "buffering" effect of American media influences by particular sociolinguistic characteristics such as those associated with Canada's Francophone cultures.[16]

Considerably less attention has been devoted to the way the international news organizations (including American) shape our general impressions of Canada as a world player, and how those treatments influence the political communications that determine various countries' independent and shared policies toward Canada.[17]

This book employs contextual analysis of the language emanating from the voices of news in order to understand the ways these voices portray and participate in Canadian/American affairs. I treat language as action and attempt to study how it is used in particular political-issue contexts.[18] This study is organized to show how news depictions of Canada as an actor in the international community have the potential to influence America's policy toward Canada.[19] The underdeveloped state of this area of inquiry in both political science and communication studies is often lamented in research.[20]

News about international affairs works as one part of the complex public discourse that informs the United States' Canadian policy. Because this study concentrates on the content of the news, it is not primarily concerned with tracing the organizational and role processes through which the content becomes news, even though the importance of organizational "imprints" on the news is recognized as one of the "blinding" elements in the process of news-shaping. Instead, attention is directed to political symbols in a variety of contextual frames associated with international relations. This approach is a response to the expressed need for a more detailed, theoretically coherent understanding of the relationship between news content and policymaking.[21] News is treated here as an internationally persuasive entity; the variation in its many forms and the range of audiences who bring specialized knowledge and levels of interest to the news enhance or detract from its ability to be persuasive. This perspective encourages questions about the relationships among persuasive forms in the news, the people who use the news, and their influence on Canadian/American relations. The main questions posed in this book are organized so that news, audiences and, specific political issues can be understood as interacting dimensions of public discourse. The questions are summarized here.

The Role of Journalism

1. What are our expectations for the role of news reporting in the evolution of foreign policy toward a specific nation, Canada, with whom we expect a reciprocal sharing of public information?

Journalism's Relationship to the State

2. How do news accounts of U.S. foreign policy behavior conform to or confront the policy objectives of the government?

The Political Orientation of the News Consumer

3. How is the individual news reader's particular political orientation to foreign affairs accommodated by news language? What audience responses for example, are encouraged by news coverage of acid rain suggesting that Canada's claims of environmental damage should be denied in favor of America's economic vitality? On the other hand, what is the likely response to this story by an officer of a major American utility that burns sulphur coal?

Portrayals of Canadian/U.S. Relations

4. How are Canadian/U.S. relations portrayed? Does the news coverage suggest that Canadian/American relations are essential to each country's well-being, or are good relations seen as convenient and part of a long-standing tradition of commerce between nations? Are these relations seen as improving or deteriorating? Is the U.S. typically represented as having the upper hand in negotiations between the two countries?

Appeals and the Political Knowledge of News Audiences

5. What are the apparent assumptions made by journalists about the audiences' level of political-historical knowledge vis-à-vis Canadian/American relations? How are these assumptions revealed in news appeals?

Arguments and Evidence in News Reports

6. What political arguments are posed by the news? How is evidence (pictures, words, interview subjects, etc.) used in the news to support the arguments that emerge?

Actors in International Affairs

7. Who are the principal actors presented in the coverage? What is the political orientation of their discourse?

Comparative News Treatment of Canada and America

8. What are the predominant, comparative images of Canada and the United States in the news? How do these images vary across domestic and foreign news organizations?

Potential Effects of News on Policy

9. What are the implications of the audiences' "readings" of this news content for Canadian/American relations?

NOTES

1. The contemporary political implications of Madison's sentiment are considered in Karp, W. (1988, May). In defense of politics. *Harper's Magazine,* pp. 41–49.
2. Baker, R. (1984, December 12). A time for Barkers. *New York Times,* p. A31.
3. Berridge, G. R. (1987). *International politics.* Sussex: Wheatsheaf Books.
4. Gwertzman, B. (1986, October 29). U.S. and Soviets weigh broadcasting exchange. *New York Times,* p. A8.
5. Ibid., A8
6. Farnesworth, C. H. (1985, March 14). Soviet-Intelsat pact raises concerns. *New York Times,* p. D5
7. Karch, J. J. (1983). News and its uses in the communist world. In J. Martin & A. Chaudhary (Eds.), *Comparative media systems* (pp. 111–131). New York: Longman.
8. Merrill, J. C., & Lowenstein, R. L. (1979). *Media, messages and men.* New York: Longman.
9. Weaver, C. (1988, November/December). When the voice of America ignores its charter: An insider report on a pattern of abuse. *Columbia Journalism Review,* pp. 36–43.

10. Holsti, K. J. (1988). *International politics.* Englewood Cliffs, NJ: Prentice-Hall.

11. Subscription appeal mailed to the author from the Christian Science Monitor Office, Boston, MA, July 28, 1988.

12. Black, E. (1988). Secrecy and disclosure as rhetorical forms. *The Quarterly Journal of Speech, 74*(2), 133–149.

13. Canada is bad news in U.S. (1985, May 25). *Toronto Globe and Mail,* p. 18. Richard Gwynn mentioned that "The American media have long been famously indifferent to Canada . . ." (p. 185). Gwynn, R. (1985). *The 49th paradox: Canada in North America.* Toronto, Ontario: Mclelland & Stewart. The fact that none of the three American television networks has a news bureau in Canada illustrates America's news myopia with regard to Canada's international role.

14. Larson, J. F. (1984). *Television's window on the world: International affairs coverage on the U.S. networks.* Norwood, NJ: Ablex.

15. Adams, W. (Ed.). (1982). *Television coverage of international affairs.* Norwood, NJ: Ablex.

16. Studies in this tradition include:

Baer, D., & Winter, J. (1983). American media and attitudes regarding government in a Canadian border community. *Canadian Journal of Communication, 10*(1), 51–86.

De La Garde, R. (1981). The media connection. *Canadian Journal of Communication, 7,* 1–27.

Elkin, F. (1975). Communications media and identity formation in Canada. In B. Singer, (Ed.), *Communications in Canada* (pp. 229–243). Vancouver: Copp-Clark.

Hart, J. A. (1963). The flow of news between the United States and Canada. *Journalism Quarterly, 40*(1), 70–74.

Payne, D., & Caron, A. (1982). Anglophone Canadian and American mass media. *Communication Research, 9*(1), 113–144.

Payne, D., & Caron, A. (1983). Mass media, interpersonal, and social background influences in two Canadian and American settings. *Canadian Journal of Communication, 9*(4), 33–63.

Petryszak, N. (1980). The nature of the Canadian television audience. *The Canadian Journal of Communication, 7,* 50–71.

Singer, B. (1975). Violence, protest, and the war in television news: The U.S. and Canada compared. In B. Singer (Ed.), *Communication in Canadian society* (pp. 611–616). Vancouver: Copp-Clark.

Sparkes, V. (1977). TV across the Canadian border: Does it matter? *Journal of Communication 27,* 40–47.

Sparkes, V. (1978). The flow of news between Canada and the United States. *Journalism Quarterly, 55,* 260–268.

Surlin, S. H., Romanow, W., & Soderland, W. C. (1988). TV network news: A Canadian–American comparison. *The American Review of Canadian Studies, 17*(4), 465–475.

Tate, E., & Surlin, S. (1976, Summer). Agreement with opinionated TV characters across cultures. *Journalism Quarterly,* 199–210.

Tate, E., & Trach, L. (1980). The effects of United States television programs upon Canadian beliefs about legal procedure. *Canadian Journal of Communication, 6,* pp. 1–17.

Trenton, T. (1984). American domination in information: Canadian student orientations. *Canadian Journal of Communication, 10*(3), 65–82.

17. Several studies are useful in this context. See for example:

Kline, S. (1981). National perspective and news bias: A comparison of national news broadcasts. *Canadian Journal of Communication, 7*(2), 47–70.

Robinson, G., & Sparkes, V. (1976). International news in the Canadian and American press. *Gazette, 22*(4), 203–218.

Scheer, C. J., & Eiler, S. (1972). A comparison of Canadian and American network television news. *Journal of Broadcasting, 16*(2), 159–164.

18. This approach is derived from Kenneth Burke's notion of symbolic action. See Burke, K. (1950). *A rhetoric of motives.* New York: Prentice-Hall.

19. A major influence within this research tradition that is concerned with the relationship of media to foreign policy is the work of Bernard C. Cohen; ". . . it would be surprising if the channels of public communication did not exert some kind of major and perhaps steady influence on the calculations of both governmental and private persons involved in the act of policy making . . . the media have become so important and powerful that they now need to be studied not as passive facilities but as active agents in the policy-making process" (p. 284). Cohen, B. C. (1957). *The political process and foreign policy: The making of the Japanese peace settlement.* Princeton: Princeton University Press.

20. "(Political scientists) . . . have yet to produce a convenient category for the press. If the making and execution of foreign policy and, for that matter, domestic policy too, can ultimately be viewed as the ceaseless expression of a political contest, then the press, ostensibly a source of information, is also a combatant, a weapon, a target and a battlefield" (p. 223). Stairs, D. (1976). The press and foreign policy in Canada. *International Journal, 31*(2), 223–243. "Despite the . . . evidence that television news content plays an important role in the foreign policy process, there remains a dearth of research into its changing role" (p. 136). Larson, J. F. (1984). *Television's window on the world: International affairs coverage on the U.S. networks.* Norwood, NJ: Ablex.

21. ". . . there is a requirement not only for factual information, but for theoretical premises and contexts that give meaning to the "facts," and for subsequent analysis that draws out their consequences and implications" (p. 7). Cohen, B. C. (1963). *The press and foreign policy.* Princeton: Princeton University Press.

PART I

NEWS MEDIA AND INTERNATIONAL RELATIONS: THEORY AND METHOD

Chapter 1

A Theoretical Framework

American foreign policy consists of rules and strategies for international action. These are generated through a complex system of communication processes that cut across diverse political orientations. One aspect of this system consists of the selective representation of policy issues in the mass media as public, political discourse. Although the ideal news perspective for representing foreign policy in western democracies is one that reveals the details of policymaking, a host of political realities constrain the full disclosure of the foreign policy process—among them, the language of the news itself. Conventions and presentational forms peculiar to the variety of news types have a tendency to interact with and transform foreign policy behavior.[1] The result is that news-mediated public discourse about international relations includes a broad range of interpretations of foreign policy and strategies for conducting it. In the collection of analytical models used to characterize foreign policymaking, the role of the media is given only superficial treatment. The media dimension of these models typically lacks theoretical and conceptual rigor. The result is a relatively unrefined synthesis that limits our ability to explain and predict foreign policy processes. For example, most of the concern for the function of the media is centered in the democratic-pluralism and bureaucratic models. This theoretical locus for the news media within foreign policy paradigms perpetuates the idea that the media operate at the level of the undifferentiated mass and routinely supports the accompanying conceptual cliché of media and public opinion as the essential communication pair in policymaking. In addition to being an idealized oversimplification, this view tends to discourage the creative exploration of the role of the media in other

3

foreign policy models. For example, there is typically little serious attention given to the role of the media in the human behavior model. This model is concerned with such matters as the psychological characteristics of egocentric power brokers; the influence of "groupthink" on policy and the exaggerated role of individual behaviors. Questions about the role of the media in contributing to Ronald Reagan's or Pierre Elliot Trudeau's policy successes and failures or about the role of the media in encouraging or repressing public discourse about the privatization of foreign policy by the National Security Council are not encouraged within the scope of this particular model. Likewise, discussions based on the international politics model of foreign policymaking suffer from the lack of a sophisticated interpretation of the role of the media as part of that model's orientation.[2] Policy interpretation tends to borrow the shop-worn, overgeneralized pluralistic notions of mass media that continue to be rigorously debated and refined in the literature of communication research. The foreign policy models of political science are not informed by the ongoing work in news analysis and conversely, much of the analysis of news discourse is politically naive.[3]

The limited research dealing with the role of the mass media in the foreign policy process suggests that less than 1% of the population make public policy or directly influence it. This research encourages us to believe that the elite hold an insidious monopoly over the media, for they are the leading players, the "stars" of international news coverage. The news reporters and their cameras in Washington participate in pseudo news events, "standupers," and other news rituals in order to capture the words of the foreign policymakers. As a result, the media help the policymakers close the loop of influence by reporting what they say and imprinting that world view on public opinion. Public opinion polls are then used to reveal public support for the policy that originated with these same policymakers and was subsequently delivered by the mass media. This is a view of the communication process in which the elite version of international reality is legitimated through the press and becomes a part of the definition of world affairs to the public. The process is considered to be circular and self-confirming for the foreign policy elite. This all happens in a strange communication ritual that leaves the bulk of the public with the impression that they have, somehow, participated in the process of policy making. But this view is too dismissive and exclusive. I suspect that its explanation of the media–policy relationship, although rhetorically efficient, underestimates the complex ways that news influences international relations.[4]

From its public relations posture, the U.S. government assigns both security and policy functions to its international diplomacy efforts.[5] The formal assumptions guiding American public diplomacy define international communication as carefully designed communication policies, themselves a subset of a larger foreign policy plan, that become manifest in communication strategies and public communication activities. Actually, political relations among nations operate beyond this idealized view that sees only carefully constructed plans of government policymakers moving through centrally controlled channels of formal diplomacy. Those familiar with behind-the-scene accounts of U.S. foreign policy processes, as revealed in the 1987 American Congressional Iran-Contra Hearings, realize that such a formal perspective ignores the reality of informal political communications and thereby restricts the development of meaningful policy strategies. One obvious oversight of this viewpoint is the tendency to see foreign policy as unified and solidly representative of a national perspective. This is a particularly misleading assumption in the case of Canadian/American affairs.[6] Another blind spot in foreign policy models based in the idea of centralized control is the failure to understand the idiosyncratic ways that audiences use the news media. The latter point is of primary interest to the work of this book.

International diplomacy both follows and determines foreign policy. As an essential concept in international relations, diplomacy requires a broad definition that includes publics and governments interacting through a variety of media forms. But the term *media diplomacy,* currently in use, is itself too simplistic; it tends to isolate and overstate the role of mass media in foreign policy. To be politically practical, the study of mediated international relations should be sensitive to the specific arrangements and shared histories that exist among nations as well as to the role of the media in initiating, perpetuating or threatening those relationships. This book assumes that Canadian/American specialists would be better informed about the policy role of the media if they looked beyond isolated news stories and their quantitative characteristics. The alternative proposed herein is a perspective for understanding the significance of a variety of news forms over time involved in the larger ongoing public discourse that informs Canadian/American relations. For example, American news reports give the general impression that most Canadians were willing to commit part of their geography and some of their international reputation to the testing of U.S. cruise missiles because, as the news put it, "Canada's terrain closely resembles that of the Soviet Union." The apparent logic of such reporting can only be judged in a context beyond the news. America's testing of cruise missiles over Canada represents much more than a static bilateral decision by elite government officials in the two countries. It is the product and active subject of a complex, ongoing, international political discourse. It is the result of the interaction of bureaucracies, historical precedent, messages, media, and publics, that together have influenced, and continue to influence, the two governments. The characteristics and implications of news reports of the cruise missile testing are considered in chapter 6 of this book.

Although interpretations of the function of news media in Canadian/ American relations vary, the news is typically granted a significant role in this particular drama of foreign affairs. The following example illustrates this tendency:

> Reagan was not admired by Prime Minister Trudeau or the media. The storm of protest over the American request to test the Cruise missile in Canada was as much an expression of fear over President Reagan's bellicosity as it was a rejection of nuclear missiles. (p. 68)[7]

In studies of Canadian/American political relations the idealized pluralistic model of press/policy relationships is dominant.[8] There is an entrenched belief that our government's policies are mediated by the press. Typical of this approach is a hypothesized interaction of four dimensions that together contribute to American foreign policy. These dimensions are the bureaucracy of the government, including the primary decisionmakers referred to as the elite; the organized, politically motivated groups of publics, variously referred to as attentive publics or opinion leaders, who are described as specialized audience groups who make it their business or avocation to follow international affairs closely; a hypothesized but poorly defined role for public opinion; and the mass media themselves, especially as represented by news and journalistic operations.[9] The kinds of communications involving these elements are described as diplomacy, intelligence, propaganda, public information, or cultural relations. Partridge, for one, challenged this model by proposing that political control resides within the selective use of communication strategies that win "support and approval":

> Only the naive now entertain the model of a political system in which policy initiatives proceed from the body of the citizens and the function of government is to give the effect to the popular will. For a great number of empirical reasons we recognize that the politics of complex societies cannot work like that; that political and other organizations, leaders and elites, bureaucracies and governments necessarily assume such functions as selecting and defining issues and problems, assembling and distributing information, proposing policies and advocating them, engaging in public persuasion, demonstrating the satisfactoriness of general lines of policy by initiating practical measures that are seen to work. . . . These are among the ways in which governments (and other influential political organizations and groups) may forge, consolidate, and expand the approval or support which enables them to continue to enjoy and deploy authority—or, as we commonly say, manufacture consent. (p. 265)[10]

Nonetheless, recent studies of Canadian/American relations reveal how the implicit communication theory of media pluralism is used to account for the state of Canadian/American relations. The following example illustrates that tendency and demonstrates the extent to which historical evaluations of international political competence are associated with presumed political functions of press coverage:

> Quite clearly, the striking thing about the Cuban missile crisis in Canada was the unanimity of support for President Kennedy and condemnation for Prime Minister Diefenbaker. The press and the public believed that both men had been tested and that the Canadian had been found wanting. "The main lesson to be drawn from all this," one official in the privy council office wrote, "is that when the U.S. President chooses to psychologically mobilize the American people on the occasion of a serious threat to them, the Canadian people will be drawn up in the process also. (p. 56)[11]

Here, both "testing" of the government leaders and "psychological mobilization" of citizens are presumed to have been mass mediated processes.

As we have seen, both the U.S. government's perspective and the research of political historians and international communication specialists suggests that there is the entrenched belief, that among western democracies, specifically between the United States and Canada, the mass media provide a necessary forum from which citizens are informed about and indeed contribute to the arena of foreign policy. The task of understanding the interaction of news with policy is further complicated by the widely divergent interpretations of this process.

QUIET DIPLOMACY VERSUS ACTIVE PUBLIC DISCOURSE

Some policy analysts who firmly believe in the process of behind-the-scenes "quiet diplomacy" are apparently so put-off by the garrulous language and popular trappings of news presentations that they propose a confounding effect for news media in Canadian/American Relations.

> In the 1980's the spotlight of media publicity has made quiet diplomacy much more difficult. It is inevitable that politicians' self-congratulatory messages, intended for a domestic audience, will be seen and heard in the other country. Similarly, conciliatory messages addressed to the foreign audience will also be received in the home country, where they will be criticized as a "sell-out."

Paradoxically, this same observer attributed a pluralistic political function to television news as discourse:

In addition to transmitting the statements of public figures however, the media in both countries often play an important role in initiating differences—or contributing to solutions. By their editorial judgment on what subjects to cover and what perspectives to adopt, the media can structure the agenda of public awareness and shape public perception of issues. The critical coverage of the NEP by the *Wall Street Journal* and other business publications, for example, had a powerful impact on public opinion in both Canada and the United States. (p. 17)[12]

It is often difficult to assess the preferred role for news in western democracies from such analyses because the ideals of quiet, behind-the-scenes diplomatic maneuvers based in interpersonal communications among the elite are counterposed, in antagonistic terms, with the ideals of the adversarial, activist press. And this evaluation is based on the assumption that news-mediated public opinion is the essential communication process for foreign relations. Rather than isolating the two communication dimensions in an unnecessarily confrontational way, the alternative, followed here, is to conceive of policy as the product of the interaction of interpersonal and mass communication processes.

MEDIA PLURALISM AND THE COMMUNICATIONS DEBATE

The Press and Public Opinion: The Point of Presumed Consensus

United States government agencies, along with those of many other governments, operate under the assumption that foreign policy success is inextricably tied to mass-mediated public opinion. The USIA perspective is reflected in these formal statements:

> International events are increasingly played out, and their outcomes shaped, in the arena of world public opinion.

> Put simply, instant global communications are breaking down rigidities and isolation, and public opinion is increasingly influential in shaping foreign policy. (p. 10)[13]

The extent to which audiences use the media in order to understand, react to, and satisfy public opinion is a recurring but intangible theme in the media and foreign policy research. As I have indicated, most observers believe that the news media are brokers of power between citizens and government.[14]

It is obvious that the concept of public opinion and the political power associated with it are problematic for the communications researcher. The usefulness of public opinion research for understanding the influence of mass communication on international politics is often questioned.[15] Philip Converse found that for most of the population below the level of the elites there is little consistency among political beliefs and opinions. "Opinions are inconsistent with each other and they vary randomly in direction during repeated trials over time."[16] Another view is that ". . . opinion research reflects the pointlessness of trying to ascertain and measure opinions of people about issues that have little salience or meaning for them except the salience created by the measurement effort itself" (p. 5). This view concludes that public opinion is more a symbol than a fact.[17] Although there are serious questions about the nature of public opinion in the research, public opinion is apparently perceived as "real" by policymakers, for it is routinely a part of their appeals as represented in news coverage. They invoke it to legitimate their policy decisions. Appeals made to public opinion in the language of news represent an important part of the discourse under review here. Therefore, this study treats public opinion as symbolically significant for policy judgments despite the problems it represents for those researchers who seek to verify its validity as a quantifiable, independent concept.[18] In this study, I treat appeals to public opinion as political language, but at the same time, question the tendency in the research to organize most explanations of media influence on foreign policy around the concept of public opinion and the explanatory models with which it is associated. But the concept of public opinion is only the floating debris of a much larger sea battle among political communication specialists; the debate over pluralistic explanations of political communications. Although I cannot review the entire scope of the theoretical confrontation in this particular study, the major points in the ongoing debate about pluralism in American political communication are addressed so that the rationale for the approach used here can be seen in a larger theoretical context.

What is the nature of the negotiation that brings together the apparently disconnected elements represented in personal political communication on one hand, and on the other, the impersonal, largely ceremonial mass communications about international politics? This question is at the heart of the debate between the critical studies scholars and those who operate from the tradition of American behavioral research. It is this particular debate that will shape the future of the study of global political communications. The two positions can only be roughly sketched here.

Some adhere to pluralism as a theory of political communication. Pluralism assumes that all citizens have a political opinion to share from their specialized cultural positions, and that they are sufficiently connected with centers of power and communication to insure that their opinions participate in a normative consensus that influences the direction of the national government. The mass media knit the various audience strata in this model, which allows the consensus to develop. The media eventually report consensus through a variety of references to public opinion. This process is presumed to occur despite a range of styles of communication involvement, levels of political sophistication, and opportunities for access to news channels. One researcher, uncomfortable with the generalized notion of pluralism, isolated the problem as a paradox:

> The paradox of mass politics is the gap between the expectation of an informed citizenry put forward by democratic theory and the discomforting reality of a low level of political awareness and knowledge in the mass electorate. (p. 3)[19]

He confronted the paradox with survey research, and proposed an alternative: A public consisting of three strata, each, from the top down, less politically active than the next. His optimistic alternative explanation to pluralism offered a kind of firehouse model of political responsiveness, with the attentive serving to waken and energize the other two floors of occupants toward political response:

> The great majority of the population lie between these two extremes and monitor the political processes half-attentively, but they can be alerted if fellow citizens sound the political alarm. (p. 186)[20]

One of the problems with this alternative is that the audience remains warehoused by virtue of a generalized, descriptive dimension that reflects little about the nuances of individual communication behavior.

The Critical Studies Challenge

The behavioral research myopia associated with most pluralistic explanations is challenged by those who assume the critical media studies perspective. They assert that the model of power and influence used in behavioral research, however framed, is essentially pluralistic because:

> pluralism assured that no structural barriers or limits of class would obstruct this process of cultural absorption: for as we all "knew" America was no longer a class society. Nothing prevented the long day's journey of the American masses to the centre. . . . (p. 60)[21]

At the core of the critical approach is a concern for the way mass-mediated messages constrain rather than accommodate political action.

Behavioral media studies are sometimes indicted for overlooking this dimension of political communication, for instance,

> since the message was assumed a sort of empty linguistic construct, it was held to mirror the intentions of its producers in a relatively simple way. It was simply the means by which the intentions of communicators effectively influenced the behavior of individual receivers.
>
> . . . conceptually, the media message, as a symbolic sign vehicle or a structured discourse, with its own internal structuration and complexity, remained theoretically wholly undeveloped. (p. 61)[22]

This perspective is skeptical of political analysts who are blind to the premises and assumptions that underlie mass communication practices. The critical studies assumption is that these dimensions communicate even more profoundly and enduringly in a political sense than the surface sounds and images of television news, for example. The basis of this brand of analysis is the search for the meanings imbedded in deep structures of discourse. Stuart Hall's description of the evolution of this approach reveals the significance of ideology as a guiding concept and the roots of Marxist criticism from which critical studies springs:

> The move from the pluralist to the critical model of media research centrally involved a shift from a one- to the two- and three-dimensional models of power in modern societies. From the viewpoint of the media, what was at issue was no longer specific message injunctions, by A to B, to do this or that, but a shaping of the whole ideological environment: a way of representing the order of things which endowed its limiting perspectives with that natural or divine inevitability which makes them appear universal, natural and coterminous with "reality" itself. This movement—towards winning of a universal validity and legitimacy for accounts of the world which are partial and particular, and towards the grounding of these particular constructions in the taken-for-grantedness of "the real"—is indeed the characteristic and defining mechanism of "the ideological." (p. 65)[23]

For cultural studies, *ideology* replaces *public opinion* as the theoretical lighthouse guiding political communication research. But the audience dimension remains conceptually, theoretically, and operationally adrift in both of the perspectives with which these concepts are associated.[24]

NOTES

1. For example, the TV network display of the images and sounds of documentary footage as concurrent, running commentary behind a reporter's spoken words represents a combination of rhetorical proofs; a potential synthesis of political meaning, that is comparatively specific to television news.

2. For a comparative review of the major analytical models for the study of foreign policy see Brewer, T. L. (1986). *American foreign policy: A comptemporary introduction* (2nd ed.). Englewood Cliffs, NJ: Prentice-Hall.

3. For a provocative critique of the rhetorical analysis of political discourse in the mass media see Joslyn, R. A. (1986). Keeping politics in the study of political discourse. In H. W. Simons & A. A. Aghazarian (Eds.), *Form, genre, and the study of political discourse* (pp. 302–338). Columbia, SC: University of South Carolina Press. Joslyn believes that political discourse is important for what it reveals about specific aspects of political life; the rhetor's world view, the rhetor's behavioral intentions, the locus and intensity of political conflict, the locus and legitimacy of political power, and the role of the public.

4. The politics that infuse foreign policy are sufficiently complex to include unexpected international communication elements. For example, news reports amidst programs that broadcast the repeated strains of American popular music bursting forth 24 hours a day from U.S. commercial international short-wave radio stations lend their own special blend of influence to the world's cultures. For details of this particular phenomenon see Browne, D. R. (1988). International commercial radio broadcasting: Nation unto nation. *Journal of Broadcasting and Electronic Media, 30*(2), 195–212.

5. "Public diplomacy is indispensable to our national security and the achievement of U.S. foreign policy objectives" (p. 4). From *United States Advisory Commission on Public Diplomacy, 1986 Report.* (1986). Washington, DC: U.S. Advisory Commission on Public Diplomacy.

6. For a discussion of this tendency see Sigler, J. H., & Doran, C. F. (1986). Twenty years after: Change and continuity in U.S.–Canadian relations. In C. F. Doran & J. H. Sigler (Eds.), *Canada and the United States* (pp. 231–249). Englewood Cliffs, NJ: Prentice-Hall. (See especially p. 232.)

7. Granatstein, J. L. (1985). Cooperation and conflict: The course of Canadian–American relations since 1945. In C. F. Doran & J. H. Sigler (Eds.), *Canada and the United States* (pp. 45–68). Englewood Cliffs, NJ: Prentice-Hall.

8. Almond and Powell offered one description of how the democratic–pluralistic model operates:

> The emergence of the mass media in a society provides the political elites with a tremendous potential for arousing the interest and influencing the attitudes of the citizens. By the same token, the free circulation of information through a mass media structure creates a great potential for popular action on the basis of widespread and accurate knowledge about political events. Independent mass media offer the average citizen opportunities to express his grievances and to call upon both the leaders and his peers to join him in seeking change. By enabling all groups and political elites to present their cases to the public in a direct and economical fashion, the media can check and regulate the performance of all political functions. In the democratic West, the freedom of the press has long been held to be integrally linked to the maintenance of free government. (p. 170)

See Almond, G. A., & Powell, G. B., Jr. (1966). *Comparative politics: A developmental approach.* Boston: Little Brown.

The two models typically represented are the democratic model in which government elites appear responsive to public opinion and the press serves as the representative of the public; the elite model, on the other hand, proposes a government elite which seeks to isolate itself from the pressures of a mass public that is not really concerned with foreign policy matters. In this model the press is represented as serving the interests of the elite by legitimating their decisions to the public, in fact the press is part of the elite group according to this interpretation. (p. 244)

Soderlund, W. C., & Wagenberg, R. H. (1976). The editor and external affairs: The 1972 and '74 election campaigns. *The International Journal, 31*(2), 244–254.

9. Hughes offered a variation on this audience-centered conception of the public audience that is more accommodating to international communication research because it is concerned specifically with audience responses to foreign policy issues. He proposed that 30% of the public constitutes the "mass public" who have very low levels of knowledge about international affairs beyond the most dramatic developments. Their opinions are poorly informed and very inconsistent. A larger group, perhaps 45%, constitute the attentive public. These are people with some general knowledge of international affairs, but their knowledge is not deep, their attitudes are not very consistent and the intensity of their views is weak. Opinion leaders, on the other hand, have high levels of knowledge about international affairs, hold consistent views, and their attitudes are held intensely. Although this group includes 25% of the population only 1% to 2% of them are active in public affairs. Hughes, B. B. (1978). *The democratic context of American foreign policy.* San Francisco, CA: Freeman.

10. Partridge, P. (1971). *Consent and consensus.* London: Macmillan.

11. Granatstein, J. L. "Cooperation and conflict," p. 56 (see note 7).

12. Leyton-Brown, D. (1985). *Weathering the storm: Canada–U.S. relations, 1980–83.* Washington, DC: The C. D. Howe Institute Toronto, Ontario, and National Planning Association.

13. *United States Advisory Commission on Public Diplomacy: 1986 Report* p. 10 (see note 5).

14. "Members of the public are more often pawns of power than independent holders of it. The media more often expedite than frustrate the control of elites as a class over the rest of society's political ideas." Paletz, D.L., & Entman, R.M. (1981). *Media, power, politics* (pp. 195–196). New York: The Free Press.

15. Benjamin Ginsberg, for example, contended that the management of public opinion by governments is a game of participatory deception and that opinion polls, specifically, are subtle instruments of the rulers in power. He pointed out that our elections only elect leaders, they do not allow us to participate directly in government policy. Ginsberg, B. (1986). *The captive public: How mass opinion promotes state power.* New York: Basic Books.

16. Converse, P. E. (1964). The nature of belief systems in mass publics. In D. Apter (Ed.), *Ideology and discontent* (pp. 206–261). New York: The Free Press.

17. Edelman, M. (1971). *Politics as symbolic action* (p. 5). Chicago: Markham.

18. Paletz and Entman concluded that "The media have five effects of public opinion; they stabilize prevailing opinions, set priorities, elevate events and issues,

sometimes change opinions, and ultimately limit options" (Paletz & Entman, Op. Cit., p. 189).

19. Neuman, W. R. (1986). *The paradox of mass politics*. Cambridge, MA: Harvard University Press. (See especially pp. 3 and 185.)

20. Neuman, Op. Cit., p. 186.

21. Hall, S. (1982). The rediscovery of "Ideology": Return of the repressed in media studies. In M. Gurevitch, T. Bennett, J. Curran, & J. Woollacott (Eds.), *Culture, society and the media* (pp. 56–90). New York: Methuen.

22. Hall, "The rediscovery of 'Ideology'," p. 61.

23. Hall, "The rediscovery of 'Ideology'," p. 65.

24. For a discussion of the tendency for content-based critical studies to exclude the audience dimension from media analysis see Fejes, F. (1984). Critical mass communications research and media effects: The problem of the disappearing audience. *Media, Culture and Society, 6*(8) 219–232. For a related discussion of Stuart Hall's treatment of the audience in critical studies see Barton, R. L. (1987, November). *An assessment of Stuart Hall's work as a way of understanding the role of mass media in foreign policy making*. A paper presented to the annual meeting of the Speech Communication Association, Boston, MA.

Chapter 2

News Form and Audience Orientation: An Alternative Approach to the Analysis of International News

The private citizen, beset by partisan appeals for the loan of public opinion, will soon see, perhaps, that these appeals are not an appeal to his intelligence.
— Walter Lippmann[1]

An alternative to pluralistic-based, quantitative news studies is proposed here. Although it borrows liberally from the critical studies concern for the form and context of meaning, it pursues the audience dimension more aggressively. It is an approach that is comparatively more concerned with the strategic implications of the individual news users' political judgment than is typical of either behavioral or critical studies research.

In the course of the analysis of this news sample, the potential influence of news language was assessed within the interactive dimensions of audience orientation and news form. The news language used to report international affairs is subject to the judgments of the politically involved people who attend to the news and eventually attempt to influence, make policy or react to decisions on the basis of those judgments. All the while, the public-at-large is a witness to and a potential participant in the process. The complexity of this process can only be partly accounted for in this study.[2]

NEWS FORM

The assumption here is that meaning results when people confront news constructions, wherever that occurs; in the news production room, in the living room of a foreign policy specialist or an environmental activist. Given the backgrounds, social positions, group affiliations, interests, and objectives of the news consumer these meanings are seldom the same. News constructions, in the course of their symbolic packaging, presentation, and interpretation have the potential for both positive and negative implications with regard to Canadian/American relations. The objective here is to reveal the shape and potential influence of these factors. The theoretical posture proposed here is a synthesis that entails negotiation of the following extremes typical of current research in news language:

> A) A symbol's meaning is not inherent in the symbol but rather in observers and their social situations. There is no objective political reality from which symbols can divert attention. (p. 200)[3]

> b) . . . these internal factors—i.e., the rules of symbolic presentation—are always there, and they constitute an autonomous phenomenon. (p.16)[4]

The first adheres to an audience-based perspective. The second is hyperformally situated and assumes that meaning resides in and is directed by the news form in the texts of political discourse.

The formal aspects of symbolic constructions in news, when studied in isolation, can lead to a kind of vacuous hyperanalysis that appears to have little bearing on political reality. On the other hand, overlooking journalistic conventions and linguistic rules can lead to conclusions that ignore a significant level of meaning in international communication; the meaning that resides in principles of news language construction. The method of analysis used here acknowledges the operation of form in a context of sociopolitical reality by demonstrating how a body of news data has the potential to engage people in polysemic discourse about Canadian/American relations. News form and the individual news "reader" are in a dialectical relationship.

> The work of establishing new kinds of "knowledge" about problematic features of social or political life is accomplished through the mediation of language; the transactions of public language are the specific *praxis*—the praxis of public signification—through which such new "knowledge" is objectivated. The relationship between this "knowledge" and its social base "is a dialectical one." (p. 276)[5]

News Voices

The term *voice* is used to identify the range of elements, including people, words, images, and sounds, selected to participate in news discourse about

Canadian/American affairs. The dimension of the news voice was analyzed by asking the following questions:

1. Who are the actors?
2. What are the voices they use?
3. What do they say?
4. What are the policy implications of what they say?

The concept of voice as it occurs in news texts is here assumed to be a complex construct of political language. The voice articulates language through narrators expressing points of view that are sometimes their own, as in news commentary, or at other times the points of view of the institutions or groups they represent.[6] Voices have the potential to generate a range of meanings. Because meaning is determined by a user's political--social orientation, it would be naive to assume that the news organizations' intended meanings are the politically significant ones for any or all audience groups. Therefore, these questions were not asked in isolation but were framed in terms of the broader historical–political context of Canadian/American relations of which the news is but one interacting element.

As part of the method, individually expressive voices were separated from their formal, presentational voices. A news voice was not assumed to be always a politically disassociated objective voice. For example, in American television news, a news anchorperson, by virtue of news conventions, has an expressive role. He or she is the authoritative, presumably informed, credible guiding voice through which world events are shared according to understood, normatively governed, journalistic conventions. But, looking beyond this presentational news role, I asked such questions as "How does a news commentator's words about national security combine with pictures of Canadian demonstrators to cast a negative light on Canadian political activity?" In order to understand the rhetorical subtleties of the voices in the news, and to reflect the range of ideological postures and political constituencies that public voices are routinely required to represent in a the arena of public discourse, a distinction was made between the actual expressive roles and the formally assigned political points of view they are assumed to represent. For example, I decided whether in a particular news context the Secretary of State's response to news about a controversial Justice Department ruling reflected his role as Secretary of State or as party/administration advocate, or both. Similarly, there are instances in the sample in which news anchors reveal a personal response to an issue. Such responses constitute subjective commentary and violate the expected convention of objective journalism for that particular context. I organized the analysis so that I could account for ways in which the interaction of these multiple-voice levels for each news participant combine to construct political reality.

In the news examples there are voices representing the news organization; reporters, commentators, anchors. There are recruited voices such as man-on-the-street responses to a certain Canadian political demonstration. There are voices of attentive groups who are highly motivated toward political action, such as those representing environmental groups who insist that American action be taken against acid rain, or that the cruise missile should not be tested over Canada. There are elite voices—Senators, MP's and Ministers—who do not, in fact, speak only as official government representatives. And there are such voices from outside the expected Canadian/American political establishment; subjective American, Chinese, and Soviet journalists whose political language represents unusual dimensions in the context of news about Canadian affairs. From the combined voices, there emerge Canadian and American national images and images of the Canadian/American alliance that have currency in international political discourse.

News Appeals

The method of analysis used here reflects an attempt to understand the specific ways news language invites political responses among citizens or discourages further discourse about issues dealing with Canadian/American relations. It involves separating the various appeals made to publics, accounting for the larger international political contexts of which the appeals are a part, associating the appeals with the voices from which the appeals emerge, and postulating a political use of the appeals on the basis of the comparative orientations of the audience.

News appeals are essentially rhetorical expressions representing the orientations to policy assumed by the news coverage. They are the leading edge of arguments for particular ideological perspectives on Canadian/American relations. For our purposes, these appeals can be described in terms of the political constituency they invite into the discursive frame and by the ways they define political issues and actors as "legitimate" players. Wolfe assessed this process of normative symbolic framing as follows:

> There is a very sharp distinction in the public domain between legitimate interests and those which are absolutely beyond the pale. If a group or interest is within the framework of acceptability, then it can be sure of winning some measures of what it seeks, for the process of national politics is distributive and compromising. On the other hand, if an interest falls outside the circle of the acceptable, it receives no attention whatsoever and its proponents are treated as crackpots, extremists, or foreign agents. (p. 266)[7]

News consists of a range of appeals that includes uncontested, nondiscursive authority (government authority, scientific authority, etc.) at one extreme and, at the other, appeals to an idealized audience, a constituency within which reside the ideals of social order in an open, participatory democracy.

This analysis recognized a range of news appeals that can be constructed and "read" separately or in combinations.[8] They include:

- Authority—appeals to uncontested, authority. Government authority is the typical example. These appeals tend to close-off, limit political discourse. Appeals to American nationalism are typical of this category.
- General Public—appeals to the unseen generalized, nondiscursive public. Vague references to public opinion are examples of this type.
- Community guardians—appeals to the sense of community needs and values; depending on the context, the appeals can refer to local neighborhoods or to the ideal of the "international community."
- Groups—appeals that are invitational to groups with highly organized goals and roles constituting a distinctive political "culture," with high levels of knowledge about specific issues and countries, that are motivated and energized through intense interpersonal group communications focusing on political issues. For example, such appeals might be inviting to environmental activists and elite policy groups concerned specifically about the acid rain problem.
- Individuals—appeals to the individual's political conscience, and sense of political commitment perceived as the requisite obligation for participating in the society-at-large.
- Ideal social order—within this appeal dimension reside the ideals of a social order involving an open, participatory democracy. These are at the opposite extreme from appeals to authority, for social-order appeals encourage political discourse about policy across audience orientations and across national boundaries.

Appeals often appear in combined forms in news discourse. In the acid rain coverage, for instance, appeals based in references to Canadian public opinion (general public appeals) were combined with appeals to censure the government for inhibiting international freedom of speech about the issue (ideal social order appeals). Appeals are also combined with a host of other rhetorical elements including invocations, metaphor, and proofs, all of which contribute to arguments about policy. Appeals were used here as a way to identify these arguments. The concept served as a point of organization and focus for the analysis of the linguistic features of the discourse. Appeals to publics were evaluated by understanding the multiple role characteristics of the voices as political actors, and by systematically identifying which in both the formal (i.e., news form) and contextual (arena of international relations) configurations, was operating in the discourse of a particular news story.

AUDIENCE ORIENTATIONS

The variety of appeals in the news have different political implications according to the orientation of the news audience. It is simplistic to suggest for example, that positive appeals to individual conscience regarding Reagan's acid rain policy would be read by all audiences in ways that encourage the continuation of that policy. The persuasive potential of meanings encouraged by the news is negotiated through a range of audience orientations to issues. The essence of political meaning emerges when audiences "read" news appeals from their idiosyncratic political orientations. Within this conceptual scheme, it is possible to consider how an individual's interpretation of the meanings in news has the potential to lead to political action, especially as that meaning becomes part of political discourse among issue-oriented groups. Bakhtin's description of the dynamics of mediated discourse cogently captures the sense in which individual news judgments can drive the discourse of political action:

> Understanding and response are dialectically merged and mutually condition one another . . . language, for the individual consciousness, lies on the borderline between oneself and the other. The word in language is half someone else's. It becomes "one's own" only when the speaker populates it with his own intention, his own accent, when he appropriates the word, adapting it to his own semantic and expressive intention." (pp. 282, 293)[9]

This study tries to steer away from the tendency in news research to develop audience categories from which media behavior is generalized without regard for the active negotiation by audiences as they confront the form of news presentations and the particular issues presented. Instead, the news user's relationship to news is portrayed in this study as a varying and dynamic interaction involving the individual's orientation to specific political issues, the appeals in news language, and their relation to his or her political culture.[10]

The Politically Active Communicator As a Point of Focus

In order to establish an anchoring point and a basis for comparison, this analysis selectively works through the audience orientation of politically active news consumers as one of a theoretically limitless range of orientations. This orientation assumes consumers whose level of knowledge about and involvement in particular issues associated with Canadian/American affairs is consistently high. The discourse associated with political influence among and between issue-oriented groups in the society-at-large and the bureaucrats and policy elite responsible for setting policy is the communication forum around which the analysis was organized. Examples that vary from this particular orientation are so indicated in the discussion.

The media used by the politically active, we are told, tend to be the specialized press and the prestige media. The popular press (and this dimension includes television news) is generally assumed to serve the needs of the undifferentiated mass audience. However, such use attributions can be misleading, for they often presume that politically active people use media only for purposes of informing themselves about the political wisdom of their peers. In fact, the concern of the policy elite for the climate of opinion and the general public mood, leads them to use less specialized media, such as network television news presentations, and to use them in ways that are more characteristic of audience orientations other than those generally associated with politically active persons.[11] One of the obvious limitations of existing conceptions for news media audiences is the failure to allow for the likelihood of role shifts in people's media-use behavior and for concurrent multiple-role activities while using the various media.

For example, the so-called policy elite are likely to use media for information about political issues that do not exclusively relate to their professional roles. Similarly, politically influential people are likely to use news for entertainment in ways that are usually attributed to the uninformed mass. And politically active publics, in the course of their symbol foraging, might politicize content that on its surface is not political. They might, for example, read foreign policy significance into stories about multinational corporation exploits in third world countries on the prime-time American TV drama series "Dallas." Models that encase people into monolithic audience compartments on the basis of hypothetical categories of media content overlook complex and variable media behaviors that combine to form a person's political culture. They also deny the relationship between media use and its influence on group recruitment and formation. Shibutani's rendering of the communicative power residing within groups as distinctive cultures offers a more realistic perspective from which to understand mediated political communications:

> Modern mass societies, indeed, are made up of a bewildering variety of social worlds. Each is an organized outlook built up by people in their interaction with one another; hence (sic) each communication channel gives to a separate world. . . . Each of these worlds is a unity of order, a universe of regularized

mutual response. Each is an area in which there is some structure which permits reasonable anticipation of the behavior of others, hence, an area in which one may act with a sense of security and confidence. Each social world, then, is a culture area, the boundaries of which are set neither by territory nor by formal group membership but by the limits of effective communication. (p. 566)[12]

Political Judgment of News Consumers

People who are politically active are likely to use news about international affairs in a selective, discursive way to make informed judgments that will influence their actions. Their media use is inherently political. Beiner's insights about the process of judgment based on a spectator's activities is illustrative of both the process studied here and the perspective from which it is studied:

> The function of the spectator is to interpret, to understand, and to judge. If we are not mistaken, these activities of understanding and judging the "drama" of human affairs are at the very heart of political experience, of what it means to *be* political. This renders an "ontology of politics" that looks to language, understanding and judgment as jointly constituting the ontological medium of political life. (p. 161)[13]

Beiner also lent support to the contention offered in this study that politically motivated viewers who are informed about particular issues from a variety of information sources have the capacity to use news reports in selective ways that deny the bedazzled political disorientation or "misrecognition" typically suggested by the critical school of media research:

> The person of exemplary judgment possesses a certain detachment from the issues being judged, and thus is not swept up into the immediacy of passion and prejudice that often attends pressing political issues. And yet he/she must also possess long and rich experience in the circumstances and context, temporal and spatial, that give to the affairs being judged their particular shape or contour. (p. 163)[14]

Judgment, then, is the essential cognitive activity a person brings to news that allows him or her to negotiate political meaning and its influence. Edelman pointed to the significance of rational judgment for political meaning in language by making a clear distinction between observation and perception of political fact. In making this distinction, he seemed to recognize the demeaning consequences of communication research that overlooks the significance of the role of the individual audience member's judgment.

> A perception of political fact is the keystone of a structure of beliefs rather than an observation; the same news accounts therefore generate contradictory factual premises. The widely propagated view that news reports can be more or less objective accounts not only converts the interpretation of news into fact but reduces the viewer/reader to objects . . . they are encouraged to relinquish their analytical faculties. . . . (p. 204)[15]

Therefore, it is fair to say that political meaning resulting from attending to news is a negotiated discourse. Polysemic news constructions are negotiated through informed judgment; judgment that is consistent with one's political cultures. The judgment of concern here rests in the politically active viewer's ability to make the distinction between the meaning of a news report for the public at large, for the foreign policy community, and for his or her role in the policymaking process. The ability to make these distinctions and to organize responsive discourse are the first steps in political action. Recent research suggests that policy-oriented audience members who are capable of engaging a news story in an argumentative, challenging discourse, are less likely to accept news definitions or news-determined agenda-setting for foreign policy.[16] Others have argued that selective and informed uses of television news by those who are politically oriented differ significantly from uses generally attributed to people who are not so politically tuned.[17]

Critical judgment of news content extends beyond the act of news consumption; it has implications for the interpersonal dimensions of political discourse that are significant parts of the daily lives of the politically active news consumer. Some believe that, in recognition of this actively engaged foreign affairs audience, specialized news forms should be developed. Cohen, for example, found the "mask of objectivity" surrounding most international news reports to be an unnecessary exaggeration of journalists' concern for balance and argued that news routines that include increased subjective analysis and correlation of international affairs are more consistent with the needs of the informed international news audience.[18] Similarly, Davison argued for a "principle of economy of effort" that involves giving the foreign affairs news audience "special attention" (p. 29).[19] But it is important not to overstate the sophistication with which those who are politically active confront media symbols compared to other audience orientations, for the politically active are also subject to and an active part of general public discourse.[20] The way news forms encourage or discourage individuals from participating in public forums that enable diverse political (national and international) constituencies to engage in political discourse about specific issues is a logical focal point for international communication research.

News and Policy Bureaucrats: Media-Used and Media Users

Policymakers treat the news as an important public opinion forum; a stage for public discourse, no matter how superficial that discourse, that demands and receives the attention of the public and other policymakers and politically active groups. The fact that most policymakers organize their political communication on the basis of the power of public opinion requires us to adjust our analysis to that reality. Apparently, policymakers are not aware of or persuaded by the arguments of media scholars who hold that media pluralism based solely on the idea of news-mediated public opinion constitutes a primitive communications perspective. Often the term *policy elite* is used to describe the decisionmakers and their bureaucratic subcultures, and to a degree, their bureaucratic function. I have argued that isolating news audiences within one-dimensional media-use categories overlooks the complexity of each policymaker's individual symbolic culture that exists beyond his or her occupational world. However, in addition to idiosyncratic individual uses, certain normative, routine, formalized uses of news by specialized groups in their day-to-day policymaking cannot be overlooked in political communication analysis.

Therefore, the analytical scheme proposed here recognizes that American policymakers tend to do their work by appealing to what they understand, in their cultures, as public opinion. These policymakers then measure their successes by opinion polls and journalistic definitions of a "prevailing public mood," despite the comparative blindness of these measures to the complex, individual judgments that politically active people bring to their communicative behavior.

As mentioned earlier, there is the suspicion in previous studies that the closed circle of news sources and news presentations for international issues in Washington leads to a "party-line" phenomenon. The fact that a large percentage of the totality of foreign affairs news generated by U.S. news organizations uses Washington, DC as the primary setting rather than a locale within the country that is the subject of the report is a recurring demonstration of this news myopia.[21] Although policymakers tend to use the prestige and specialized press for the bulk of their international affairs news, they also use television news as part of their occupational routine to understand the political climate, the strategies of their colleagues, friends, and foes alike in foreign policymaking spheres. One common assumption in media and foreign policy studies is that although most people do not attend to news about international affairs with near the attention and frequency of the specialists involved in policymaking, their attention is deemed significant in that it has the potential to contribute to a vaguely defined "public mood" to which the policymaker must be attendant and responsive for purposes of political expediency if for no other reason.[22] The interpretation of this public mood is significant. It presumes the existence of audiences within discrete, unconnected audience categories. The so-called "attentive minority" is seen to be set against the "apathetic majority" when foreign affairs issues gain saliency. The assumption is that the attentive minority, those who routinely follow foreign affairs, are less likely to be influenced by government or the mass media, whereas the apathetic majority will follow the government's lead.[23] And it is assumed that policymakers use news to state their opinions, make appeals to public opinion, float trial balloons, and undercut other agencies engaged in foreign policy with which they disagree. Consequently, even though the TV networks' coverage of international affairs is often characterized as little more than thumbnail-sketch-sensationalism for the mass audience, one should not dismiss the policy implications of this news, for it can constitute a significant definition of political reality for policymakers.

INTERNATIONAL POLITICAL ACTION AND INVITATIONAL DISCOURSE: THE CONVERGENCE OF NEWS FORM AND AUDIENCE ORIENTATION

Politically active people may read news presentations as arguments for a policy of isolation and confrontation on one hand, or, on the other, as invitations to develop, defend, and participate in policies that work toward international cooperation. News appeals are, in effect, politically significant disclosures of the attitude of each particular news voice toward the public's legitimate discursive role in America's relations with Canada.[24] There are a number of interpretations of the significance of an individual's media use for international relations. Among them is that those who routinely use the media from a politically active orientation tend to be more secure in their national identification and, as a result, are more likely to reach out and identify with foreign groups as well.[25] Another thesis contends that media coverage showing a balance of power between the nations portrayed is likely to contribute to a trusting relationship.[26]

Invitational discourse in news reports can contribute to a person's political activity. As I have suggested, the degree to which one confronts news with political intentions depends on the "reader's" orientation to specific issues, and the importance of a particular report to the political culture of which he or she is a part. It is not simply a case of the journalist's intended meanings being serendipitously attractive and useful to the "reader." Journalistic accounts can be invitational when people establish a discourse with news that constitutes a meaningful process of coorientation involving their judgment and the formal characteristics of the news. One or both of the following conditions bring news texts and the reader into a discursive relationship:

1. The rhetorical construction in the news is ideologically and syntactically persuasive.
2. Individuals who use the news adopt strategies of appropriation; that is, they selectively read news texts (an "oppositional reading" is one example) in ways that enhance their own political discourse within their political cultures.

The idea that news media forms might offer discursive "invitations," although not systematically developed as theory, is found in research about the role of the media in social change. Chaney pointed to the political significance of media discourse that is invitationally barren:

> [T]he public is now distanced as a set of onlookers whose opinions may be mobilized although the cultural form does not invite participation. . . . [(It)] offers an attitude to public life in which the charismatic role of leadership comes to supplant all informed debate, and eventually political dramas become purely fantastic: "fascism thrives on fantasy, while democracy has grown up with science and recognition of newly noticed facts." (pp. 133–134)[27]

Similarly, working from the assumption that media use is part of the dialectic between the individual and society, Dahlgren viewed news presentations as encouraging either "reflexive or non-reflexive consciousness" where:

> Reflexivity would make it possible for the viewer to consider, in a practical and normative way, alternative possibilities to present social circumstances. The reflexive consciousness is one which learns from its own shared social experiences—from its own history—to contemplate the present in a critical way . . . a non-reflexive consciousness, on the other hand, is conceptualized as an object of history. Such a consciousness does not see itself as a participant in the construction of the social world; it sees itself as merely acted upon by the social world. (p. 104)[28]

As a first step in evaluating the usefulness of the perspective outlined here, I identified the comparative potential of news forms, when confronted by a person's critical judgment, to invite a political response; whether that respondent is a conservative status-quo policymaker or an activist determined to change government policy. There can be a variety of responses about which we can only speculate; from subtle interpersonal recognition of an issue that might be filed away for later use, to appeals that, in association with other information sources and interpersonal contexts, might lead to active collaboration, recruitment, and the development of political strategies to achieve a particular policy objective.

Politically active individuals have been known to combine interpersonal and public communications beyond their national borders in inventive ways. International political networks have evolved among Canadians and Americans to achieve specific political objectives. In fact, it was just this kind of transborder communication among Canadian and American citizens that was responsible for the creation of the International Joint Commission, the environmental policy organization that is the oldest and most respected of all of the permanent joint commissions of Canada and the United States.[29]

"Disaggregation" is political communication that, in essence, constitutes a "divide-and-conquer" strategy.[30] Often, attempts to achieve a "dual coherence" between domestic and external policies confound the communications required to achieve mutually advantageous goals among nations and their many constituencies. Through transnational disaggregation, bureaucrats and interested publics alike attempt to circumvent the inflexible, focused control inherent in formal state bureaucratic relationships.

Transnational public communications, especially between Canada and the United States, have a long history. They are generally viewed as quite effective, but threatening to the control exercised by established national governmental power centers. Canada is seen as being a superior "disaggregator" in Canadian/American affairs because "it's easier to politicize matters in Ottawa than in Washington, easier to break them out of their compartments, . . ." (p. 232).[31] Transnationally negotiated policy initiatives and responses to policy constitute a significantly different rhetorical milieu from domestic responses. Tucker's description of such enterprises is enlightening:

> Public internationalism on the part of spirited Canadians has long been most profuse and intense within the Canadian/American relationship. The cross-border collaboration by like-minded Canadians and Americans has been aimed at influencing the decision-making process of "disaggregation." One of the functions of Canada may be to precipitate into international discussions points of view held by many Americans but not accepted by the administration for support. (pp. 18–19)[32]

Understanding the potential influence of news reports on "public internationalism" between Canada and the United States is a major objective of this news analysis, and the investigation of the role of invitational discourse in that international context shapes the remainder of the book's organization.

Invitational Coorientations

Appeals in the news and one's judgment from a particular political orientation represent the essential forum for mediated transnational public political discourse. For it is at this dialectical juncture that political action is invited or dismissed. Four types of invitational coorientation are proposed for illustrative purposes. They represent points around which news discourse and politically active people might converge and, in so doing, activate the discourse of public internationalism. Several coorientations might be used concurrently for any policy issue; they are not proposed as mutually exclusive concepts. They are organized in a way that reflects their potential to invite transnational discourse (from most likely to least likely) for politically active news consumers.

Disjunction. Disjunction is a coorientation that facilitates judgment expressing alternatives to existing political arrangements and processes. The news can present information previously unknown to the politically active news audience, including foreign policymakers. This news takes the form of leaks, trial balloons, challenges from competing government agencies, from foreign governments, public opinion response to significant issues and late-breaking developments that have not yet found their way into formal channels of communication.[33] There are a variety of situations in which information presented in the news has the potential to work against the entrenched interests of those organized for international political action, whether they are government bureaucrats, lobbyists, or interested citizens. The news consumer, in this case, is relatively disoriented by or "blind" to this information because it originates beyond the communications and control parameters of his or her political cultures. The live interviews with Lebanon's Nabih Berri during the TWA hijacking crisis; the Cronkite interviews with Egypt's President Sadat prior to the Camp David Meetings during the Carter Administration; and Pierre Trudeau's asides to reporters after his peace initiative meeting with President Reagan are examples. Significantly, vital political information to which certain constituencies may be "blind" can be out of the control of both the news producers and the policymakers. For the contextual mix of foreign and domestic news voices, audience predispositions and the developing political issues themselves combine to make meaning in an organic way that is beyond the intentions, expectations, and immediate awareness of those who routinely exercise communications control in foreign affairs.[34] The coverage of the National Film Board issue reviewed in Chapter 5 is a clear example of a news confrontation that generates organic meaning for and about the participants in unexpected ways. The disjunction coorientation, compared to the other three types, is likely to be more invitational for those outside formal policymaking circles, as in the case of citizens interested in transnational communications about specific issues.

Internationalization. Some news appeals are framed in an international forum, using a mix of international images, voices, and languages to present issues of concern to Americans in the context of the international community. These reports can be organized within a broad range of possible journalistic controls over the international context; some include foreign spokespersons who define the issue, others selectively represent international images while using the field reporter and domestic politicians or military authorities to introduce, define, and otherwise interpret the issue at hand. The extent to which these reports provide "other-culture" insights through which Americans might enlighten their understanding of international affairs determines the relative transnational communications potential of this coorientation.

Domestication. This coorientation type involves news consumers negotiating international news that is framed in domestic contexts. Appeals to nationalism constitute a recurring example. Simply excluding information about international reaction to a particular policy is implicit domestication on the part of a news agency. For example, the administration in power might mount a campaign through the news media to define an external threat to American interests from abroad. If the news selectively displays a show of consensus supporting this definition among foreign policy leaders, and, meanwhile fails to provide information about the response to this definition from the world community, the nationalistic definition might prevail. In certain situations, the definition of an external "threat" might be exaggerated in order to enhance domestic political power, or to divert attention from domestic or foreign issues that threaten the credibility of the administration in power. The Reagan Administration's aggressive, public discussion of the threat Grenada posed to U.S. interests prior to the 1983 American invasion of that island has been interpreted by some as a case of news media-assisted hyperdefinition of the communist threat for Reagan's political gain. This point of coorientation offers the potential for volatile political discourse about definitions of foreign versus domestic policy and about the relative priority of international versus national issues.

Public Accreditation. News coverage both reflects and manufactures the image of "the public." Some news, as a response to foreign policy issues, encourages the citizen-activist, lobbyist, or government policy specialist to use its reporting as a barometer of public opinion and, perhaps more significantly, to rely on the news as the primary credible source for that measure. News invocations of public opinion typically argue for responses that are imbued with the "public interest." News formulas routinely include public interest appeals in their constructions to satisfy normative expectations about the "public service" role of journalistic enterprises rather than to seriously present detailed information about the pros and cons of a foreign policy issue. These formulas are also used by politicians to demonstrate that they are effectively representing their "publics" by invoking the "public good" as part of the rationale for their support for particular policies. The result is a coorientation that confronts the reader with predictable, standardized news packaging of public interest appeals replete with generalizations and oversimplification of complex international issues. This coorientation offers comparatively less invitational promise than the others for the politically active news consumer interested in transnational communications.

NOTES

1. Lippmann, W. (1922). *Public opinion.* New York: The Free Press.
2. Edelman described this analytical dilemma provocatively:

a student of the international scene has constantly to take account of three analytically distinct modes of political interplay which influence and compliment each other. There is the political bargaining area in which formal governmental organizations make policy respecting international affairs, but always in response to the demands and sanctions of interested groups which have something tangible to gain or lose. There is the mass public of political spectators, to whose powerful influence the direct participants must always be sensitive, but who are mobilizable in support of particular questions, especially militant ones, or rendered quiescent through identifiable psychological and political processes. Finally, there is the bargaining, largely tacit, among group interests in rival countries, which is a major source of the domestic bargaining power of these interests. (p. 170)

Edelman, M. (1971). Op. Cit., p. 170.
3. Edelman, M. (1985). *The symbolic use of politics* (p. 200). Urbana, IL: The University of Illinois Press.
4. Roeh, I. (1982). *The rhetoric of news radio.* Bochum, West Germany: Studienverlag Dr. N. Brockmeyer.

5. Hall, S. (1974). Deviance, politics, and the media. In P. Rock & M. McIntosh (Eds.), *Deviance and social control* (pp. 261–305). London: Tavistock.

6. For a discussion of this particular notion of the concept of *voice* as an element in discourse see Chatman, S. (1978). *Story and discourse.* London: Cornell University Press.

7. Wolfe, R. P. (1965). Beyond tolerance. In R. P. Wolfe, B. Moore, & H. Marcuse (Eds.), *Critique of pure tolerance* (pp. 3–52). Boston: Beacon.

8. This conception of appeals is my interpretation of a typology offered by Duncan. Duncan, H. D. (1968). *Communication and social order.* London: Oxford University Press.

9. Bakhtin, M. M. (1981). *The dialogic imagination.* Austin, TX: The University of Texas Press.

10. Morley has found that people respond to news presentations in idiosyncratic ways that defy class-bound conceptions of media audiences:

> my own research shows plenty of examples of selective perception, rejection of dissonant messages and a distinctly cognitive orientation to the medium on the part of working class groups, with an equally complex set of responses and interpretations on the part of the middle class groups in the sample. (p. 29)

Morley, D. (1980). *The nationwide audience.* London: British Film Institute. One study specifically directed at understanding the role of media in Canadian/American relations found no support for American media imperialism effects on Canadian audiences, and concluded that the audience member's culture is a key factor in understanding the political power of media. Social background was found to be a stronger predictor of attitudes, agendas, and information acquisition than interpersonal or media exposure. These researchers argue that interpersonal and sociolinguistic variables should be incorporated in media effect studies in order to give a more realistic understanding of media effects. Payne, D, & Caron, A. (1983). Mass media, interpersonal, and social background influences in two Canadian and American settings. *Canadian Journal of Communication, 9*(4), 33–63.

11. See for example, Davison, W. P. (1974). *Mass communication and conflict resolution: The role of the information media in the advancement of international understanding.* New York: Praeger.

12. Shibutani, T. (1955). Reference groups as perspectives. *American Journal of Sociology, 60,* pp. 562–569

13. Beiner, R. (1983). *Political judgment.* London: Methuen.

14. Beiner, Op. Cit., p. 163.

15. Edelman, 1985, Op. Cit.

16. Iyengar, S., Peters, M. D., & Kinder, D. (1982). Experimental demonstration of the "not-so-minimal" consequences of television news programs. *The American Political Science Review, 76*(4), 848–858.

17. See, for example Meadow, R. G. (1980). *Politics as communication.* Norwood, NJ: Ablex. See especially chapter 5, "Modes of Political Participation." Similarly, Bennett and Edelman argued that too much research has focused on the individual as target for mass mediated politics and that we should instead now

consider "how people in collectivities can best present and reconcile competing truths" (p. 162). Bennett, W. L., & Edelman, M. (1985). Toward a new political narrative. *Journal of Communication, 35,* 156–171.

18. Cohen, Op. Cit., 1963.

19. Davison, 1974, Op. Cit., p. 29.

20. "Though government officials and other elites make conscious efforts to manipulate mass opinion, these are not our chief concern. Far more influential are the mobilizations of both elite and mass political opinion that stem from their engagement with the same symbols. Sometimes, governmental actions or language create distrust in official policy, and information from new governmental sources can reinforce or counteract official cues" (p. 10). Edelman, 1971, Op. Cit., p. 10.

21. Indeed, the earlier conclusions about media influence on foreign policy were based on this limited perspective. Cohen described the circularity of the foreign policy process:

> Both Walter Lippman and, thirty years later, Gabriel Almond have pointed out that "The American people as a whole do not make foreign policy decisions affecting their survival in any direct sense; that there are steep gradations of interest and competence in foreign policy within the American public; and that one's relationship to information-both as consumer and producer- is in large part a function of one's position in this policy-making structure. (pp. 5–6)

Cohen, Op. Cit. 1963, pp. 5–6. Larson supported the notion of a closed system of policymaking:

> The policymakers who most directly affect the foreign policy of the United States not only utilize the content of network television news, but also influence and contribute to that content in several ways. News conferences or briefings at the White House, State Department, Pentagon or on Capitol Hill are usually certain to generate network television coverage. Larson Op. Cit., 1984, (p. 136).

Recent communication analysis suggests that this is an exaggeration of the media's role in the policymaking process.

22. For a discussion of this idea see Davison, Op. Cit., p. 19.

23. Davison, 1974, Op. Cit., p. 22.

24. For a discussion of invitational form in TV news see Barton, R. L. (1986, Spring). Foreign policy implications of CBC-TV coverage of Canada's international affairs. *The Mid-Atlantic Journal of Canadian Studies,* pp. 87–101.

25. Buchanan, W., & Cantril, H. (1953). *How nations see each other.* Urbana, IL: University of Illinois Press.

26. Davison, 1974, Op. Cit., p. 47.

27. Chaney, D. (1981). Public opinion and social change. In E. Katz & T. Szecsko (Eds.), *Mass media and social change* (pp. 115–136). London: Sage.

28. Dahlgren, P. (1981). TV news and the suppression of social reflexivity. In Katz and Szecsko Op. Cit., p. 104.

29. For a discussion of the history of the IJC see Willoughby, W. R. (1979). *The Joint Organizations of Canada and the United States.* Toronto: The University of Toronto Press. (See especially pp. 40–41.)

30. This discussion reflects the concepts introduced in Dickerman, C. R. (1976). Transgovernmental challenge and response in Scandinavia and North America. *International Organization, 30*(2), 213–240. See also Griffiths, F. (1971). Transnational politics and arms control. *International Journal, 26*(4), 640–674.

31. Dickerman, Op. Cit., p. 232.

32. Tucker, M. (1980). *Canadian foreign policy: Contemporary issues and themes.* Toronto: McGraw-Hill, Ryerson.

33. "The ability of the mass media to reach decision makers directly offers a valuable, if limited, means of short-circuiting the bureaucratic network and partially alleviating the isolation of top policy makers. At the White House and at lower levels of the government it is common for officials to learn about a particular event or idea from an item in the mass media and then to ask subordinates to explore it further. The ability of the press to introduce new ideas into the decision making process is particularly important since many bureaucrats are reluctant to rock the boat" (pp. 17–18). Davison, 1974, Op. Cit., pp. 17–18.

Cohen pointed out that even top-level policymakers are very dependent on mass media for their information about international affairs. Cohen, Op. Cit., 1963, p. 209ff.

Stairs suggested that there is a greater tendency for the Washington policy elite to engage in such press manipulations than there is in Ottawa. He also pointed to several specific uses of mass media materials from which we can generalize: "Policy makers may sometimes attempt to influence the expectations of their opposite number in an international negotiation, or manipulate the domestic environment within which they function, by leaking to the press in advance pertinent statements of attitude, intent or capabilities" (p. 234). Stairs, D. (1976). The press and foreign policy in Canada. *The International Journal, 21*(2), 223–243.

34. Accounting for the interaction of conventional and organic form in the making of political meaning is consistent with the argument offered in this book that by virtue of informed judgment the artistic (that is, inventive and unconventional) use of news forms is politically significant because it can be politically invitational. Barton and Gregg made the following points about this dimension of news form:

> Historically form has been considered within one of two general conceptual frameworks. First, there is what might be called conventional or technical form, which refers to artificial presentational or shaping devices that are imposed upon content to give it the quality of discreteness. Second, there are essential formative principles that are intrinsic to the content and grow organically within it to imbue it with unique characteristics of formed meaning. Aspects of conventional form can be easily identified and studied in television news. They are the result of the kind of technology employed and the production decisions to be made with regard to how certain stories are to be presented. Thus we can refer to shot composition, video mix, dramatistic

format, the personalizing of issues, and the justaposition of news stories. The components of organic form are more difficult to delineate. The distinction between conventional and organic form was clearly stated by Samuel Taylor Coleridge over a century ago:

The form is mechanic, when on any given material we impress a predetermined form, not necessarily arising out of the properties of the material; as when to a mass of wet clay we give whatever shape we wish it to retain when hardened. The organic form, on the other hand, is innate; it shapes as it develops itself from within and the fullness of its development is one and the same with the perfection of the outward form. Such as the life is, such is the form.

It may be, then, that "form" in television newscasting has not yet been adequately accounted for because the *distinction* between conventional and organic form, rather than their *intermingling,* has guided the explication. (p. 174)

Barton, R. L., & Gregg, R. B. (1982). Middle East conflict as a TV news scenario: A formal analysis. In *Journal of Communication, 32*(2), 172–185.

PART II

The Politics of American News in Canadian/American Relations

Chapter 3

The Historical Context of
Canadian/American Relations

Everytime we deal with the Americans we lose our Shirts.

—Horwood[1]

Historically, America's involvement with Canada in the international arena can be characterized as a series of short-term bursts of activity driven by apparently self-serving objectives.[2]

Although Canadian and American international objectives have tended to be similar, American interest in and support for Canada's international activities pales when compared to Canada's diplomatic and media investment in America's domestic and international policies and actions. The American response, or lack of it, is often explained away by Canadians and Americans alike as attributable to the vast differences in international power and responsibility between the two countries. Recently, political scientists and economists have confronted this explanation with the America-in-decline thesis, which proposes that certain middle-power countries, among them Canada, are prepared to move into the international power vacuum left in the wake of America's decline in prestige and power in the international community.[3] As we see here, the American news coverage does not routinely reflect the view of a declining America in its treatment of Canada's international affairs, but certain international news sources actively support the idea of America-in-decline relative to Canada, and aim their appeals at world audiences accordingly.[4]

TRADITIONAL ISSUES IN CANADIAN/AMERICAN RELATIONS

There are specific issues associated with Canadian/American relations that appear to be timeless. These issues are accompanied by traditions of political posturing in the arena of public discourse on the part of Canadians and Americans alike. Sigler and Doran made the point that the Canadian/ American agenda has remained essentially the same since it was articulated by Canadian diplomat Hume Wrong in 1927. Points of conflict in Canadian/American relations mentioned by Wrong that are significant for this study include:

- Canada's different international commitments,
- Tariff policies,
- U.S. exploitation of Canadian natural resources,
- U.S. resentment of Canadian programs of conservation,
- Canadian domestic legislation that could be represented as confiscatory of U.S. capital,
- The greater tolerance of Canadians for public enterprise, which might be interpreted as Canada's "socialistic and radical" character,
- The impact of American broadcasting,
- The Canadian's misunderstanding of the "cumbrous machinery" for directing foreign affairs in the United States, and
- The absence of executive responsibility in Congress.[5]

POLITICAL CHARACTERISTICS OF THE TRUDEAU–MULRONEY–REAGAN ERA

Most of these features were a part of the texture of Canadian/American affairs for the 1983–1989 period from which our news examples were chosen.[6] They occurred within a dramatically changed North American political atmosphere. For example, the Reagan administration's goal of reestablishing America's power internationally was the dominant political influence on the North American agenda for 1983–1984, the period in which "Canada was in the U.S. doghouse" (p. 249)[7]

From its narrowly defined nationalistic vision, the administration's response to Canada was tempered by the comparative philosophies and political styles represented in the transition between Canadian Prime Minister Trudeau and Mulroney. Trudeau's response to the escalating U.S./Soviet tensions associated with the Reagan administration's foreign policy was to renew Canada's internationalist intermediary role, most dramatically displayed in his peace initiative.

Many believed that the Mulroney government represented a significant change for Canadian/American relations when it took power in the fall of 1984. Mulroney's style was captured in the Shamrock Summit metaphor and his salutation to the Americans on September 24, 1984 that "Good relations, super relations, with the United States will be the cornerstone of our foreign policy" (p. 32).[8] Mulroney's enthusiasm was dampened considerably amidst charges by Canadian political observers that his administration had succomed to the Reagan administration's tendency to swagger through international relations for domestic political gain. The Reagan administration's response, or lack of it, to Canada, during the period has been interpreted from the Canadian viewpoint as a beneficial shock for Canadians in the long run because it had the effect of jarring them from their complacency which had subjected them to restrictions and a level of control from the United States that were becoming intolerable.[9] The significance of journalistic forms for Canada's relations with the U.S. during the period are captured in Clarkson's recommendation that:

> Were Canada to adopt a more comprehensive strategy towards the United States, the role of communicating its aims and programs would be crucial to the strategy's success. If it were met with the same misinformed anti-Canadian editorial opinion as greeted the NEP (National Energy Policy) it would trigger the same pressure for retaliation which gives Canadian mandarins nightmares. (p. 319)[10]

Early in this period Canadian/American relations were influenced on the Canadian side by a highly concentrated power structure under Trudeau with a less-than-open attitude toward the United States. The lack of improvement in relations was further complicated by the nature of the differences in government structures and processes in the two countries. There were Canada's federal-provincial power struggles on one hand; and on the other hand, the all-too-familiar U.S. complex executive-legislative arrangement involving a multitude of decision-making points for every foreign policy issue. Members of Congress tend to shape their foreign policy decisions on the expressed needs of their domestic constituencies. Because this is a time-consuming process, U.S. government negotiations with Canada are often left stalled and fractured.[11] In response to the U.S. tendency to domesticate its foreign policy processes, Canadian Ambassador to the U.S., Allan Gotlieb defined his modus operandi in a speech in November 1983:

> No country inevitably becomes so much engaged in the domestic process of another country as does Canada in that of the U.S. This is because Canada is so greatly affected by U.S. domestic legislation and regulations. Thus a great deal of U.S. foreign policy towards Canada is not really its foreign policy at all, but its domestic policy. And we, whether we like it or not, are drawn into the American domestic process. (pp. 249–250)[12]

More recently, optimistic predictions for significant improvements in Canadian/American relations, especially in the area of free trade, have been tempered by the realization that the history of the relationship has nurtured powerful nationalistic fires in both Canada and the United States that could confound the promises of the Shamrock Summit rhetoric.[13] Free trade as a political communications issue is reviewed in chapter 7. Political commentators assume that the formalized institutional ties between Washington and Ottawa can handle the problems that arise between them, and that these communications are sufficient to bind and sustain Canada and the United States in a "Pluralistic security community" (p. 439).[14] The way the activities and policies of those institutional ties are reported in the news and the extent to which they involve the Canadian and American publics are of concern to this study. Canadian sovereignty is at the heart of the matter. The extent to which journalistic political discourse defines, maintains, alters the perceptions of Canada's association with the United States in light of international public scrutiny is a major communications issue for future Canadian/American relations. Holmes summarized the political tension that confronts the journalists who would report on Canadian/American affairs:

> If we slip into regarding ourselves primarily as two associated North American states, then I think we are faced with frustration and impotence, as well as confused and angry arguments about loyalty. In that kind of harness we are bound to be wagged by the tail. (p. 85)[15]

The background of world politics for the period of this study against which Canadian/American affairs were being staged included a general world recession characterized by government policies of protectionism, and the seemingly spontaneous but deeply rooted evolution of world peace and environmental movements in which, not incidentally, tens of thousands of Canadians were involved.

NOTES

1. Horwood, H. (1988). Everytime we negotiate with the Americans we lose our shirts. In L. Lapiere (Ed.), *If you love this country* (pp. 115–119). Toronto: Mclelland-Stewart.

2. America's imperialistic tendencies toward Canada are recalled by Teddy Roosevelt's response to American businessmen seeking to take full advantage of northern wealth; Roosevelt aggressively pushed for and received international support for his definition of the Alaska boundary that shut off Canada's access to the Yukon. Morton, D. (1983). *A short history of Canada.* Edmonton: Hurtig.

3. For an extended discussion of this idea see Dewitt, D. B., Kirton, J. J. (1983). *Canada as a principal power: A study in foreign policy and international relations.* Toronto: Wiley.

4. A recent exception to this rule is Schmeisser, p. (1988, April 7). Taking stock: Is America in decline? *New York Times* Section B, pp. 24–27, 66–68, 96.

5. Sigler and Doran, 1985, Op. Cit., pp. 231-249.

6. For a review of the tensions in Canadian/American relations in the early 1980s see Bromke, A., & Nossal, K. R. (1983/1984, Winter). Tensions in Canada's foreign policy. *Foreign Affairs,* pp. 335-353.

7. Gwynn, Op. Cit.

8. *The Wall Street Journal* 9/24/84. p. 32

9. Clarkson, S. (1982). *Canada and the Reagan challenge: Crisis in the Canadian-American relationship.* Toronto: James Lorimer.

10. Clarkson, S. (1982). *Canada and the Reagan Challenge,* p. 319.

11. For a discussion of this point of tension in Canadian/American relations see Leyton-Brown, *Weathering the Storm,* pp. 17-18.

12. Gwynn, Op. Cit., pp. 249-250.

13. For a discussion of the significance of the 1983-1984 period in Canadian-American relations see Bromke, A., & Nossal, K. R. (1987, Fall). A turning point in U.S./Canadian relations. *Foreign Affairs* p. 169.

14. This particular view is expressed in Holsti, Op. Cit.

15. Holmes, J. (1981). *Life with uncle: The Canadian/American relationship.* Toronto: University of Toronto Press.

Chapter 4

The News Examples

A language is a dialect that has an army and navy.
— Max Weinreich (1894–1969)

The news examples included here are American television news reports, American prestige newspaper coverage, and international broadcast and print news releases. The characteristics of each form are reviewed through a range of political issues, then a comparative analysis of all of the forms for specific issues is undertaken in later chapters.

THE AMERICAN NETWORK TELEVISION NEWS EXAMPLES

Popular criticism of news coverage of international affairs routinely takes television network news to task for being limited in scope, exclusive, over-dramatized, if not down right sensational. It is also characterized as ahistorical, simplistic, and certainly biased. Television news, especially, has been identified as being less expository than typographic forms.[1] There is merit to the argument that print-based, expository prose involving judgment, deduction, sensitivity to contradiction, the ability to synthesize ideas, encourages political action. However, such an approach taken to its extreme tends to dismiss the political significance of the informed, active use of electronic news as political discourse.[2] Such characterizations probably reveal as much about weaknesses in the methods of studying news discourse as they reveal about the essential characteristics of news. Television news is a highly derivative form; it borrows shamelessly from the mass newspaper. First there was the party press; characterized by serious, opinion-forming journalism. It was used specifically to mobilize people for party objectives; it catered to a subculture of attentive, politically active readers. That party press is a distant cousin of today's network television news. Television's closer kin is the tabloid newspaper, supported by advertising, not party funds from a devoted readership. The tabloid newspaper and television news share the important characteristic of being at once both political and popular. That is, both forms are associated with national political life and power centers of society while being a primary vehicle for popular entertainment. They both pay attention to violence, crime, scandals, stars, and dramatic settings from high and low society.[3]

Isolating the formal characteristics of American television news required the examination of 2 full years of coverage. The 1983–1984 period was chosen for the initial analysis because, as mentioned earlier, it represents a pivotal period in Canadian/American relations. In addition, the analysis of American TV network news was extended through 1988 for a specific issue, cruise missile tests over Canada, as part of a cross-media comparison of domestic and foreign news treatment of Canadian/American relations.

The three American commercial network news organizations, CBS, NBC, and ABC, devoted 2 hours, 13 minutes and 30 seconds to international affairs coverage involving Canada for the 2-year period, 1983–1984 inclusively. The 96 stories (see Table 4.1) range from very brief accounts — for example a 20-second comment on the G.M. strike in Canada — to extended, special reports as long as 4 minutes and 20 seconds, about the acid rain problem. Although every story mentioning Canada was analyzed for its potential role in international relations, some were judged to have less significance in that process as it is defined in this research and were therefore not included in the analysis.[4]

The major issues covered were: acid rain, Canadian/American auto labor disputes, the U.S. Justice Department response to National Film Board documentaries about acid rain and nuclear war, the Williamsburg Economic Summit, Canada's appeals for the return of Canadian businessman Jaffee who was being held in Florida for suspected land-swindle crimes, Trudeau's peace initiative, the U.S. cruise tests in Canada, Trudeau's resignation, the Canadian elections, terrorism in Montreal and in Quebec City, the drowning of caribou, U S./Canadian drug traffic, and the Georges Bank fishing dispute.

In the TV news examples, there surprisingly are fewer instances of American government elite voices actually speaking their own words on camera than Canadian elites. This characteristic differs from the trend in previous studies.[5] Similarly, there is a greater representation of on-camera interviews with Canadian citizens than with American citizens. We might

TABLE 4.1
News Stories Involving Canada from the Three American TV News Networks
for 1983–1984 Inclusively

Item #	Date	Network	Length	Description
1.	1/2/83	NBC	3:20	Acid rain
2.	1/7/83	CBS	:20	Canada unemployment
3.	2/22/83	CBS	:40	Acid rain
4.	2/24/83	CBS	:20	Canadian films
5.	2/25/83	ABC	2:20	Canadian films
6.	2/25/83	CBS	2:10	Canadian films
7.	2/25/83	NBC	1:50	Canadian films
8.	3/1/83	CBS	2:20	Nuclear waste trans.
9.	3/8/83	CBS	:30	Canadian lumber
10.	4/17/83	ABC	2:50	Gold fever
11.	5/4/83	NBC	2:00	Toronto baby deaths
12.	5/27/83	ABC	4:30	Williamsburg Summit
13.	5/28/83	NBC	5:50	Williamsburg Summit
14.	5/30/83	NBC	4:20	Williamsburg Summit
15.	5/31/83	NBC	2:40	Nova Scotia/Agent Orange
16.	6/8/83	NBC	:20	Trudeau/Central Amer.
17.	6/12/83	CBS	:20	Canada/politics-Mulroney ousts Clark as Tory leader
18.	6/29/83	CBS	1:10	Acid rain
19.	7/23/83	CBS	:30	Canada/cruise-demo
20.	7/26/83	CBS	:40	U.S./Canada Jaffee case
21.	8/2/83	NBC	2:10	U.S./Canada Jaffee case
22.	8/7/83	NBC	3:40	U.S./Canada border-Agent Orange
23.	8/23/83	ABC	:10	Acid rain
24.	9/6/83	BCS	:40	Chrysler contracts
25.	9/25/83	ABC	:20	Thatcher visits
26.	10/5/83	CBS	:40	U.S./Canada Jaffee case
27.	10/16/83	NBC	2:50	Acid rain
28.	10/21/83	CBS	2:00	Canada/U.S. crime
29.	11/10/83	NBC	:10	AmWay Corp fraud
30.	11/18/83	NBC	4:20	Acid rain (special)
31.	12/15/83	ABC	1:50	Trudeau/peace talks
32.	12/15/83	NBC	:30	Trudeau/peace talks
33.	1/17/84	NBC	:10	Zhao visits Canada
34.	1/23/84	ABC	:30	Canadian lottery winner
35.	1/23/84	CBS	1:00	Canadian lottery winner
36.	1/23/84	NBC	:30	Canadian lottery winner
37.	2/6/84	ABC	2:10	Winter Olympics
38.	2/6/84	NBC	3:00	Winter Olympics
39.	2/7/84	ABC	:30	Winter Olympics
40.	2/7/84	CBS	:20	Canada/skating test
41.	2/15/84	ABC	:40	Trudeau in USSR
42.	2/15/84	CBS	:30	Trudeau in USSR
43.	2/15/84	NBC	:50	Trudeau in USSR
44.	2/22/84	ABC	:20	Acid rain

(continued)

TABLE 4.1 *(continued)*

Item #	Date	Network	Length	Description
45.	2/22/84	CBS	:10	Acid rain
46.	2/29/84	ABC	2:20	Trudeau resigns
47.	2/29/84	CBS	:20	Trudeau resigns
48.	2/29/84	NBC	2:00	Trudeau resigns
49.	3/6/84	CBS	:30	U.S. cruise test
50.	3/9/84	NBC	:30	Canada seal hunting
51.	4/1/84	CBS	2:40	Acid rain
52.	5/8/84	ABC	1:40	Provincial building shooting Quebec City
53.	5/8/84	CBS	1:40	Provincial building shooting Quebec City
54.	5/8/84	NBC	1:40	Provincial building shooting Quebec City
55.	6/15/84	ABC	2:40	Trudeau resignation
56.	6/15/84	NBC	4:10	Trudeau resignation
57.	6/17/84	CBS	:20	Politics/Turner
58.	6/17/84	ABC	:20	Politics/Turner
59.	6/20/84	NBC	2:00	Acid rain
60.	6/30/84	CBS	:20	Trudeau resignation/ Turner sworn in
61.	6/30/84	NBC	:10	Politics/Turner sworn in
62.	7/1/84	CBS	2:30	Machias/Seal Island
63.	7/6/84	CBS	2:40	U.S./Canada economies
64.	7/9/84	CBS	:10	Politics/Turner
65.	7/24/84	ABC	1:40	Canada's elections, Turner's sexist behavior
66.	7/24/84	CBS	2:00	Canada's elections, Turner's sexist behavior
67.	7/28/84	CBS	3:00	U.S./Canada electricity
68.	8/1/84	NBC	:20	Canadian lottery winner dies
69.	9/3/84	NBC	1:30	Montreal terrorism, bomb
70.	9/3/84	CBS	1:40	Montreal terrorism, bomb
71.	9/3/84	CBS	3:40	Canada elections
72.	9/4/84	ABC	2:00	Canada elections
73.	9/4/84	NBC	2:00	Canada elections
74.	9/4/84	ABC	:20	Terrorism aftermath
75.	9/4/84	CBS	2:10	Montreal terrorism
76.	9/5/84	ABC	:20	Canada elections
77.	9/5/84	CBS	:10	Canada elections
78.	9/5/84	NBC	:30	Canada elections
79.	9/13/84	ABC	1:40	Montreal terrorism, bomb
80.	9/17/84	ABC	:10	Mulroney
81.	9/17/84	NBC	3:20	Mulroney
82.	9/25/84	ABC	1:30	Canada/frozen bodies
83.	10/2/84	NBC	:30	Caribou kill
84.	10/4/84	ABC	1:40	Caribou kill
85.	10/3/84	CBS	2:00	Caribou kill
86.	10/12/84	CBS	:30	U.S./fishing dispute
87.	10/13/84	NBC	:40	U.S./Georges bank

TABLE 4.1 *(continued)*

Item #	Date	Network	Length	Description
88.	10/17/84	CBS	:20	Gen. Motors strike
89.	10/17/84	NBC	:30	Gen. Motors strike
90.	10/21/84	CBS	:20	Gen. Motors strike
91.	10/22/84	CBS	:30	Gen. Motors strike
92.	10/27/84	CBS	:20	Gen. Motors
93.	10/27/84	NBC	:20	Gen. Motors agreement
94.	10/29/84	CBS	:20	Gen. Motors contracts
95.	12/6/84	CBS	2:20	St. Lawrence Seaway
96.	12/14/84	CBS	3:30	Ads for kids banned

conclude from this brief comparative summary of the news voices that the Canadian perspective with regard to American policy toward Canada is substantively represented. And, following the focus of our study, we might be tempted to conclude that by attending to network news, Americans are likely to be exposed to the Canadian international political perspective. On the surface, the news appears to be fulfilling its ideal pluralistic role in the tradition of western journalism of inviting publics to review and respond to the government's policy toward Canada through the presentation of a full discourse of Canadian and American actors responding to a broad range of issues and the policy that is associated with those issues.

However, probing beyond the surface of the frequency counts of the actors and themes of the news coverage, it becomes apparent that the contexts in which the news elements are organized contribute significantly to political meaning. This organization primarily occurs through the news voice that recruits subordinate voices in much the same way a stage director coordinates stage action. As the controlling narrator, it calls up voices as required to shape meaning. This is not to suggest, however, that such manipulation leads only to meanings that are intended by the news producers; for it is the variety of political meanings negotiated beyond the intentions of the journalists that most likely characterizes the communications behavior of politically active media users. It is apparent that the identification of the comparative suasory success of appeals emanating from the range of voices in the news, including the apparently controlling voices of the news producers, can only be judged in the context of audience orientations.

THE FOREIGN NEWS EXAMPLES

The first step in selecting the international news examples was a review of news reports about Canada's foreign affairs activity for the 1983–1988 period. The Foreign Broadcast Information Service (FBIS) was the primary source of this news. One of the most frequently mentioned issues was the U.S. cruise missile tests in Canada. International news accounts of this particular issue were considerably more detailed and complex in structure than for other issues. The FBIS coverage was analyzed comparatively against other media forms including American domestic print and television coverage.

Following the method of analysis introduced earlier, the interaction of actors, issues, and voices represented in the press accounts were identified along with the particular appeals they bring to international public discourse. Those appeals were then evaluated in their contexts in terms of their potential influence on the nature and status of Canada's international relations, especially with the United States.

The FBIS—A Brief Background

FBIS is a world-wide newspaper, press agency, radio and television monitoring system, operating under the Directorate of Intelligence in the Central Intelligence Agency (CIA) of the United States. The service dates from 1941, when the Federal Communications Commission (FCC), at the suggestion of the State Department, started the service for purposes of recording broadcasts of foreign origin, translating speeches and news items, and reporting the important findings to other agencies. This intelligence service is described as "Indispensable to foreign service officers and ambassadors, U.S. diplomats, policy planners, military staffs and the American press. The service was eventually put in the hands of the CIA as a "service of common concern" (p. 32).[6]

Those who tend to be critical of the impact of CIA operations on the international political climate have raised questions about the credibility of the FBIS as a source for information on which to base policy, or for use by scholars, the press, and its public. Marchetti and Marks pointed to instances of apparent abuse of the service. They recalled examples of the CIA using the FBIS monitoring reports to check whether the CIA's own clandestine radio services are in fact reaching their targets. Those same authors found especially reprehensible the fact that the operators in the CIA's clandestine services are reluctant to reveal their propaganda operations even to their own editors, who are themselves members of the CIA's intelligence directorate. As a result, there exists the likelihood that bogus CIA radio stations (e.g., CIA stations posing as the Voice of China and sending false messages under that disguise for political purposes) would be monitored by their own FBIS editors and entered into the daily reports as legitimate radio China comment. The critics' concern is that these false reports would then subsequently be used by subscribing journalists, by academicians and perhaps even by foreign policy bureaucrats who had not been informed of that particular operation.[7] Despite the limited debate about the credibility of the FBIS reports, the fact remains that the information gathered by the FBIS *is* used by policymakers to make policy, and by journalists to report policy-related developments through the *prestige press.*

Both the American television network reports and world press opinion represented in FBIS transcripts were compared with the American press versions of the same issues in order to understand how American public discourse about Canadian/American issues is informed and/or constrained by the inclusion or exclusion of those international viewpoints. Previous research suggests that those directly involved in the making of American foreign policy use the news services reviewed here to make judgments about salient international issues, and to survey American and world public opinion about those issues and U.S. foreign policy. W. Phillips Davison pointed to the significance of FBIS reports for both policymakers and journalists:

> These monitoring reports can be considered an integral part of diplomatic reporting even though they may not be prepared by diplomats at all. Like telegrams or other messages received from embassies, they provide information about events and attitudes in other countries, and are incorporated into the process of foreign policy making . . . indeed, they constitute a major source of information for Washington journalists who cover international affairs. (p. 392)[8]

Davison reviewed the key role played by the FBIS reports in the closed-loop of political influence involving the press and the international policymaking community:

> These journalists, when they choose to make use of materials from a FBIS document, may provide a link in the chain of communication between two governments (The U.S. and The Soviet Union). Thus Moscow may beam a short-wave broadcast to North America, which is recorded and transcribed. Journalists may then prepare stories based on the monitoring report. These stories are picked up by the Soviet embassy in Washington, the Soviet news service *Tass,* or some other agency and reported back to Moscow. The Soviet government then knows that this particular message was received in Washington and may get some American reactions to it. (p. 393)[9]

Head, likewise, pointed out that news organizations often rely on official monitoring services to supply exclusive news of world events. His comments reflect the reality of rhetorical intentions associated with the selected use of international broadcasting reports and the necessity of understanding the larger political context of which monitoring discourse is a part.

Intelligence and news organizations must, of course, treat monitored reports warily because they may consist of disinformation rather than genuine information. (pp. 358–359)[10]

But, I would argue, the selective treatment proposed by Head, that is, journalists making a distinction between these varieties of information (disinformation and genuine information), is itself an interpretative process that is inherently political and one that has implications for the ways national presses constrain the potential influence of world opinion on public discourse about foreign policy.

Characteristics of the FBIS Examples[11]

The regions represented by FBIS-monitored reports about Canada's international role include: China, Western Europe, Latin America, Eastern Europe, Cuba-Caribbean, Southeast Asia, Southern Asia, Africa, Middle East, North America and Australia, and the Soviet Union. The comparative frequency of news reports for 1983–1984 by region is summarized in Table 4.2 as an example of the pattern of world press coverage of Canada. Although the quantitative ranking of reports shown in Table 4.2 provides some understanding of the shape of the news, it should be used cautiously. One should bear in mind that there are a number of variables reflected in these rankings that could be confounded in drawing political inferences. Among them are the FBIS's selective reporting from the news items from any given country, the variation of responses to particular international issues reflecting the saliency of an issue for the reporting country, and the

TABLE 4.2
Number of Reports about Canada for 1983–1984
Ranked by FBIS Regional Categories

China	147
USSR	127
Cuba & Carribean (Carribean 37, Cuba 24)	61
Latin America	52
Middle East	48
Eastern Europe	40
N. America, Australia	37
Western Europe	32
Africa	25
Southeast Asia	22
Southern Asia	22
TOTAL FOR 1983 – 1984	613

Source: Foreign Boradcast Information Service

technological capability of a country as measured by the volume of news transmissions.

Many of the reports are characterized by their preoccupation with the ceremony of visits; the international shuttle of dignitaries provides for the rhetorical occasion, the formal platform or the excuse for discussions of policy. For example, while a visit by a Soviet delegation to Canada to discuss agricultural trade clearly involves that objective, East–West tensions and the role of Canada as intermediary in missile deployment in Western Europe are the political subtexts of both the meetings and the press treatment of those occasions. Often these formal, ceremonial visits are reciprocated, completing the diplomatic ritual. For example, Trudeau's visit to Rumania is followed by a visit to Ottawa by the Rumanian foreign affairs minister.

Reports about the cruise tests, specifically, represented the most frequently mentioned single issue and these reports were, for the most part, from the press services of the Soviet Union. Taken as a whole, the FBIS examples show Canada pursuing an independent, dynamic role on the stage of international politics. For example, the Jerusalem Domestic Service reported on October 26, 1983 that Canadian Minister of External Affairs, Allan MacEachen, during his visit to Israel, criticized that country's policy in the territories, especially the continued presence of Israeli troops in Lebanon, as an obstacle to peace. And, Canada is reported as taking a tough stand against U.S. involvement in Central America (April 2, 1984). MacEachen, in talks with American Secretary of State Schultz emphasized that Canada believes that the involvement of the Contadora is the best route to peace in Central America. This is followed by a report (April 9, 1984) of MacEachen talking with government officials in Nicaragua, again supporting the Contadora process by offering Canada's assistance in peace efforts. And there is a not-so-subtle display of policy woven among the texts of this international news discourse. One example revealed how the Trudeau government played out Canadian policy toward America on the larger stage of world affairs; a perspective rarely included in American press coverage of Canada. On April 10, 1984 Trudeau announced that Canada would evaluate its position toward Nicaragua after MacEachen returned from his Central American trip. Canada, Trudeau said, would not send ships to join France's efforts to remove American-placed mines in Nicaraguan waters, thereby keeping with Canadian policy of not sending ships into danger areas without U.N. approval. This appeal reaffirmed the Canadian policy of respect for the sovereignty of nations and, by example, lent ironic force to the report from the Montreal Domestic Service of the following day, April 11, 1984 which reviewed developments in the Canadian/ American territorial waters dispute. In that report, the U.S. spokesperson claimed that jurisdiction goes back to Truman's proclamation in 1945, suggesting the dispute could disturb U.S./Canada relations. Taken together, the foreign press reports raise the question of the consistency of U.S. international maritime policy compared to Canada's. This constitutes invitational journalism for those oriented toward this issue. Implicit in that question is the nature of America's respect for both Canadian and Nicaraguan sovereignty. Awareness of this larger context of international news leads one to ask, to what extent did American journalists, in their selective use of international news releases available to them, inform their audiences about Canada's international activities and their significance for the relations between the two countries? Of some surprise, again in the comparison of this news with America's Canadian affairs coverage, was the fact that Canadian *domestic* issues routinely were a part of foreign news reports.

AMERICAN NEWSPAPER EXAMPLES

The U.S. prestige newspapers coverage of Canadian affairs (including the *New York Times,* the *Washington Post,* and the *Los Angeles Times*) for the 1983–November 1988 period were reviewed as a basis of comparison against which the other news categories were evaluated. The newspaper examples were used in several ways. They were used to compare formal categories of news construction, such as predictive form. In other instances, the newspapers were part of a detailed comparison of depth-of-coverage, relative degree of invitational discourse, and so on, against American television and FBIS news. The latter comparison is essential to the study because one of the main objectives is to understand the extent to which the U.S. press includes foreign journalistic accounts of Canadian/American relations in its own reportage and the potential influence of that news on policy.

NOTES

1. Postman, for example, argued that "a television-based epistemology pollutes public communication and its surrounding landscape . . ." (p. 28). He reviewed the meritorious characteristics of a print-oriented public discourse: "a sophisticated ability to think conceptually, deductively and sequentially; a high valuation of reason and order; an abhorrence of contradiction; a large capacity for detachment and objectivity; and a tolerance for delayed response" (p. 63). Postman, N. (1985). *Amusing ourselves to death: Public discourse in the age of show business.* New York: Viking-Penguin.

2. Nichols described film-video exposition as an involving discourse:

Exposition, stemming from rhetoric, enjoins time to support an argument or description, which is typically presented to the viewer in direct address (by characters or narrators speaking directly to the viewers). Stress falls on the sequential ordering of a logic that requires a certain duration (running-time) for its presentation but may refer to or fabricate an imaginary time of quite different dimensions. (p. 81)

Nichols, B. (1981). *Ideology and the image.* Bloomington, IN: Indiana University Press. (See also pp. 201–205 for a useful analysis of television news reportage from this perspective.)

3. McQuail, D. (1983). *Mass communication theory.* Beverly Hills, CA: Sage.

4. Several of the news stories dealt only briefly with specific Canadian issues but the contexts in which those references occurred were considered politically significant. For example, although Canada's participation in the Williamsburg Economic Summit coverage is only briefly mentioned, the news treatment of Canada is an important comparative index of American news coverage of Canada in an international context.

5. See for example, Adams, W. A., & Heyl, P. (1981). From Cairo to Kabul with the networks, 1972–80. In W. A. Adams (Ed.), *Television coverage of the Middle East* (pp. 1–39). Norwood, NJ: Ablex. See also Larson, J. F. (1984). *Television's window on the world: International affairs coverage on the U.S. networks.* Norwood, NJ: Ablex.

6. Cline, R. S. (1981). *The CIA under Reagan, Bush and Casey.* Washington, DC: Acropolis.

7. Marchetti, V., & Marks, J.D. (1974). *The CIA and the cult of intelligence.* New York: Alfred A. Knopf.

8. Davison, W. P. (1976). Mass communication and diplomacy. In G. Boyd, J. Rosenau, & K. W. Thompson (Eds.), *World politics* (pp. 388–403). (New York: The Free Press.

9. Davison, 1976, p. 393.

10. Head, S. W. (1985). *World broadcasting systems: A comparative analysis.* Belmont, CA: Wadsworth.

11. This study is to be distinguished from one that would compare Soviet and American journalism characteristics as competing forms of international discourse. That approach would be an entirely different enterprise given the fact that the Soviet press examples represent both foreign and domestic objectives while the American news examined here is primarily intended for domestic consumption. The concern of this study is how the American press monitors, selects, and incorporates international press discourse about Canadian/American relations into its reportage.

Chapter 5

A Formal Survey of American TV Coverage of Canadian/American Relations

There is always a problem that media will confuse their myths and begin to occupy their own skewed ideological frames.

— *The Nation* (p. 480)[1]

ESTABLISHED HABITS: THE FORCE OF RITUAL AND MYTH IN TV NEWS

Even in the midst of controversial issues, Canadian/American relations are typically presented as tranquil. This is the recurring theme throughout the American news examples. It is especially evident in the National Film Board coverage reviewed in detail in this chapter. For example, Frank Reynolds announced that, "Three films made in Canada, of all places, have been disapproved by the critics at (the) Justice Department" (ABC 2/25/83, 2:20).

The incredulous tone of this comment implies that our relations with Canada are trouble free, that Canadians are our safe friends. Another reporter began an acid rain story with these words: "A few years ago it would have been hard to believe that something as apparently inoffensive as rain could threaten diplomatic relations between two of the friendlier nations on earth" (NBC 1/2/83, 3:20).

And later in this same story: "The Canadians are a patient people, but they want action on acid rain, not more studies."

In a story on the Canadian elections the reporter concludes that, "Whatever happens, Canadians will continue to be our good neighbor to the north; steady, safe and reliable" (CBS 9/3/84, 3:40).

Although the dramatic tension of many of the news stories, such as those in the acid rain coverage, benefit from the suggestion that the pacific quality of the relationship may be threatened by the acid rain controversy, the mythic interpretation of the friendly, unperturbable nation to the north prevails as the dominant appeal. Americans find reassurance in the notion of a traditionally tranquil, enduring, supportive, untroublesome neighbor in the international community even if most of us know nothing about the details of that neighbor's political culture. In fact, the very presentation of detail might challenge the stereotype. The generic language inherent in news appeals that define Canada's image works to perpetuate the myths while leaving the credibility of the news unchallenged. This kind of language is essentially mythic for it not only promotes conformity but celebrates it. The language is inherently hortatory; operating at the convenience of the user to present images that serve certain persuasive objectives. One of the consistent rituals of television news is the selective construction of forms that enhance news authority and credibility. Mythic constructions are appropriate for the political discourse of news; they present certain beliefs as doctrine and the form itself suggests that the beliefs are not challengeable. However, the tranquil image of Canada is in fact not the only mythic form operating in the news. Several others are revealed in the discussion that follows.

"MONDO CANADA": SITE OF THE NEWS BIZARRE

There is a recurring TV news form that one might label "Mondo Canada," after those "Mondo Cane" films of the 1960s that parade before your eyes the bizarre and unusual; birds that fly backwards, people who eat dogs, and dogs who return the favor.

Here is an excerpt from a news story of this type:

Anchor: This sounds almost like something out of a science fiction movie. Men, preserved perfectly for more than a century, then being discovered unexpectedly in the modern world. Well, that's exactly what's happened in the arctic reaches of Canada and, let this be a warning, it is a bizarre story with images to match. (ABC 9/25/84, 1:30)

Two more examples:

Anchor: Gold fever, it has always driven men to wanting [sic] to take unusual journeys, often dangerous ones. The latest outbreak of gold fever is on a remote lake in western Canada where the search is not for gold dust but a singular, giant, 300 pound nugget. (ABC 4/17/83, 2:50)

Reporter: British Columbia is rich in scenic beauty and rich in what one man believes is a gold nugget worth 20 million dollars. That man is 82 years old Magnus Gernberg who was out on a lake one day back in 1934 and saw the wreckage of a boat. A boat with a hole in it. Thirty years later he came across a newspaper article describing an incident in 1892 involving a boat, a boat with a hole in it. (ABC 4/17/83, 2:50)

Even stories that on face value appear specifically to be about Canadian politics are cast in terms that emphasize bizarre, tabloid features. The preoccupation with John Turner's campaign practice of patting women on their fannies, and the ensuring flap about that behavior, dominated the election coverage to the extent that no political issue of import to Canadian/American relations is revealed. Similarly, two networks, ABC and NBC devoted considerable time to a review of Trudeau's political career at the time of his resignation. Both, however focused on the unusual nature of his personality characteristics ("arrogant, passionate"—NBC) and lifestyle (his failed marriage is reviewed amidst shots of Margaret Trudeau's night life—ABC, NBC). Even in this context, the Turner fanny-patting images are resurrected to define the nature of Canadian domestic politics. Trudeaumania is compared to Kennedy's camelot. More importantly, this definition of Trudeau as bizzare is used to suggest that tensions between America and Canada during his tenure can be primarily attributed to Trudeau's personality rather than to substantive political issues of concern to Canadians in general. Following U.S. Ambassador Robinson's call for Americans to be more alert to Canadian sensibilities because "Canadians bruise easy," NBC's Garrick Utley ironically and tellingly concluded his Trudeau retrospective with the comment that the lesson, for Canada, of Trudeau's American posture is that "No Canadian can ignore the colossus to the south."

These examples, along with reports about mysterious baby deaths in a Toronto hospital and of Canadian lottery winners, reveal essential elements of narrative and folk story forms. There is clearly a narrator; the language is cast in the mold of the oral tradition of story telling. The form includes ballad-like structures such as incremental repetition—the repetition of lines in such a way that their meaning is enhanced either by their appearing in changed contexts or by minor successive changes in the lines themselves. This discussion is not intended to suggest that this form has no political import for its audience. On the contrary, the form is part of a persistent flow of images that work to establish general perceptions of Canada. The communications issue involved here is whether they feed static stereotypes or realistically inform us about Canada's political–cultural behavior.

VIDEO BORDER CROSSINGS: TOURING CANADA VIA FLORIDA

The TV news locus for American citizens interacting with Canadians is Florida. This is the place where American viewers get the most frequent and detailed look at Canadians. But these particular Canadians happen to be cast as villains and are usually wrapped in unsavory issues. There is land-swindler Jaffe and a host of drug-running Canadians hiding out and threatening the well-being of Floridians. French-speaking Canadians are the focus of this particular story, which is planted in cultural stereotypes and feeds on enthnocentrism:

> Anchor: We're approaching that season when some northerners look forward to a warm welcome as they seek sun, sand, and surf at places like southern Florida. But Wyatt Andrews reports some visitors from the far north can anticipate a chilly reception in the deep south.
>
> Reporter: Besides being a "Who's Who" of Canadian mobsters, these men have one more thing in common. Each was recently arrested in South Florida. Fugitives in an area police say has become a haven for Canadian crooks.
>
> Police Representative (Bruce Nill, Florida Dept. of Law Enforcement): We have identified over three hundred known Canadian organized crime members and their associates operating and living either full or part-time in southern Florida.
>
> Reporter: Florida officials are studying what they call a rush of Canadian mobsters into the area around Hollywood, Florida. It is already called "Little Quebec" here because of the legitimate Canadian businesses that serve a million and a half French speaking visitors every year.
>
> David Lang, U.S. Customs Agent: They blend into this Canadian-speaking community. They look like any other tourist to us.
>
> Reporter: Investigators say the Canadians (note the generalization) increasingly are smuggling drugs. Richard Foley, one of Canada's notorious bank vault burglars, was arrested in a Florida hotel on cocaine charges. Two months ago, a man police described as a Canadian mob financier William Oberant was charged with being part of an international drug ring that smuggled valium into the United States for sale as qualudes. Police predict the growing Canadian pressure could spark mob violence.
>
> David Lang, U.S. Customs Agent: The Canadians are starting to get a little greedy. For one thing they're making a lotta, lotta money and the U.S. faction of the mob wants some of this.
>
> Reporter: No one is sure just how you stop this flow of fugitives; by trading Canadians and Americans across the border; by showing any single identification? There is also a language barrier. For years police in South Florida

have thought it enough if an officer spoke Spanish. Now there is a growing need for officers to also speak French. Wyatt Andrews, CBS News, Tampa. (CBS 10/21/83, 2:00)

"'Greedy' Canadians-as-criminals" is the generalization in this language. The language encourages a "we-versus-they" response that works against internationally collaborative discourse.

PRECIOUS PRESCIENCE: THE PREDICTIVE URGE IN TV's FOREIGN AFFAIRS COVERAGE

Television news tends to connect stories by predicting the outcome of the issues covered and to verify these predictions with selective supporting data. This tendency lends meanings to stories about Canadian/American relations that can influence policy makers' judgments. For example, a conflict between the two countries over environmental issues might be imbued with a prediction that Canada will accede to the United States because of unequal economic power brought to bear by the United States.[2] The form and function of news prophecy for foreign policy depends on audience orientations and requires an understanding of the way the news includes rhetorical strategies that work to enhance its credibility as a communication source. Several questions about the predictive nature of news emerge in the context of news representations of Canada: Are these predictions simply an artifact of oral tradition on which news form was developed — a part of the internal story-telling "machinery" that adds drama and lends satisfaction to the viewing process but of no consequence to the world of international political reality? Are they, like Cassandra's dire prophecies in classical mythology, essentially accurate but lacking credibility because of the source from which they spring? Or is the predictive voice more like Eleanor Porter's Polly Anna, blindly and excessively optimistic about Canadian/American relations reflecting a simplistic portrait of Canada that is typical of the bulk of the American news coverage?

Excerpts from TV's coverage of Canada demonstrate the variety of political appeals that result from television's predictive urge:

Reporter: The prospect is that in Muskoco lake and many other places in Canada and the northeastern United States acid rain will continue to fall. Robert Bissell, NBC News, Muskoco Lake, Ontario. (NBC 11/18/83, 4:20)

Anchor-Rather: No improvement (in the Canadian economy) is expected in Canada until it starts happening here (in the U.S.). (CBS 1/7/83, :20)

Reporter: If other towns in Vermont vote the way they did in Thetford, nuclear waste from Canada may be stopped. But by the mid 1980s the problem will be even closer to home when plants here run out of storage space for their nuclear waste. The problem of where that (Canadian nuclear waste) can be shipped if the public protests will probably have to be settled in the courts. Marlene Sanders, CBS news, Thetford, Vermont. (CBS 3/1/83, 2:20)

Reporter: There shall be a change on the 4th of September. Canada, as it does in most things, follows the American trends, and Mulroney follows the Reagan trend. Whatever happens, Canada will continue to be our good neighbor to the north; steady, safe, and reliable. Personalities aside, with a Reagan in Washington and a Mulroney in Ottawa North America will be a conservative continent, wall-to-wall, for the first time in more than twenty-five years. Bob Simon, CBS News, Ottawa. (CBS 9/3/84, 3:40)

Reporter: And Canadian Communication Minister Francis Fox predicts the (National Film Board) issue will be an embarrassment for the (U.S.) government. (NBC 2/25/83, 1:50)

Reporter: State's attorney Boyles filed new fraud charges against Jaffe last month which could mean many more months of legal problems. Lisa Myers, NBC News, Avon Park, Florida. (NBC 8/2/83, 2:10)

The predictions are claims. They are one of the elements in the structure of news arguments about Canadian/American relations. As undisputed truths in their individual story contexts, they gain authoritative force from the presentation of apparent "window-on-the-world" images and sounds. The issues themselves are stripped of their political details. They are most often presented in a selective, nondiscursive way. The individual predictions are transitory invocations. They are "safe" from the news point of view, for they do not challenge the political slant of the narrative constructions; they do not invite verification. They are hortatory devices that contribute more to the authority of the news than to an ongoing public discourse about the issues on which they are constructed. They are one of the constituent elements of news credibility. Unlike general descriptions of Canada as "the friendly neighbor to the north," the predictions are most often cast as active claims subjectively rendered from the reporter's authoritative voice in the context of a contested political issue. The political potency of these claims is no doubt related to the perceived credibility of the news reporter, which varies across issues and audience orientations. The predictive pattern in TV news creates a text of interacting expectations, including a continual emphasis on the future at the expense of providing a broader, historical context for the issue at hand. Viewers are encouraged by this pattern to judge events on the basis of the evidence presented by the reporter, the logic of which is often guided by a concern for dramatic clarity and simplicity that tends to exclude the untidy, provocative, and ambiguous elements that might detract from or put into question the authority and apparent efficiency of the news narrative. Ironically, verification of the predictive claims through systematic following up and presentation of proof is not part of the news routine; nor is it encouraged. Rather, the predictive claim is part of a persuasive appeal that enhances the authority of the news. The predictions can, within and among news reports, weave into the news flow mistaken expectancies and misrepresentations of the intentions and actions of people in international affairs and the political contexts that motivate and respond to their actions. In this television news, the repetition of predictive claims across stories feeds a derogatory image of Canadian dependency on the American economy and military; of Canada as a faceless legalistically bound monolith against which American citizens must contest their individual rights. Predictive claims are but one example of how television news includes apparently self-serving treatments of information about international relations. But television is not the exception; each news form barters substantial details about international relations for formal efficiency and persuasive appeal. That is the inherent blindness in all news. Therefore, news consumers require a broad range of domestic and international reportage as ongoing, public, critical discourse if we are to realistically respond to and inform American foreign policy.

OUT OF STEP AND STEPPING OUT: POLITICAL APPEALS AS DEVIATIONS FROM STANDARD NEWS FORM

Media presentations of individuals involved in foreign policy who are operating outside ritualistic, formalized meetings and addressing the media directly have greater symbolic power than communications that take place within the closed formal proceedings themselves that do not alter existing arrangements but are expected communication rituals.[3] Foreign policy elite are likely to pay close attention to such statements because they are comparatively idiosyncratic, operate outside formal channels, and, therefore, challenge the prevailing policies. Often, these are special situations in which reporters seize a spontaneous opportunity to catch an impromptu word from formal session participants. Both news producers and political spokespersons understand the nature of the opportunity and its potential for making political waves in the policy establishment. The stories dealing with the Justice Department treatment of the National Film Board documentaries demonstrate this phenomenon. In that case (examined later in this chapter) the news operated as a political voice, moving in where some

U.S. elites were in conflict and suggesting that the Justice Department was operating against the best interests of the American public.

One of the most poignant examples of Canadian "endruns" in operation was Prime Minister Trudeau's "oppositional code" uttered while he was leaving the White House after after his unsuccessful "peace initiative" meetings with Ronald Reagan.[4]

Anchor: The Canadian Prime Minister, Trudeau, is profoundly concerned about the nuclear arms race and he's been traveling the world for many weeks trying to get all the nuclear powers to sit down together and discuss how nuclear weapons can be eliminated. Today, Mr. Trudeau was at the White House and talked to the President. His message was a dialogue on arms control. Here's ABC's Sam Donaldson:

Reporter: Prime Minister Trudeau left the White House today virtually empty-handed after attempting to interest President Reagan in his peace initiative. An initiative that has already been criticized by some U.S. officials. Last night, in Toronto, Trudeau, feisty and undaunted, had called such officials "pipsqueaks."

Trudeau: . . . if some pipsqueak in the Pentagon criticizes our peace initiative, the press runs to say "oh, look they don't like what we're doing."

Report: Trudeau's peace initiative calls for a disarmament conference attended by all five nuclear nations. A different approach from the current path of super power U.S./Soviet talks. And an approach that President Reagan totally ignored in his goodbye to Trudeau today.

Picture: Reagan and Trudeau in front of the White House.

Reagan: I thank you Mr. Prime Minister for coming here, sharing your ideas with us and we wish you God's speed in your efforts to help build a durable peace.

Reporter: Disappointed or not, Trudeau made the best of it.

Trudeau: As you have just heard, the President supported what is being known as my peace initiative.

Reporter: The question of support aside what about those Pentagon critics?

Picture: Trudeau walking to waiting limo with President Reagan and his cabinet; the camera reveals Schultz and Weinberg, stern-faced, intently listening to Trudeau's remarks to the press.

Trudeau: Third-rate and third-level pipsqueaks who say that I'm not allowed to talk about peace because somehow we haven't pulled our weight in NATO. That is baloney; to use a polite word. (ABC 12/15/83, 1:50)

Trudeau's reception during this visit must have been a painful contrast for him compared to his very successful U.S. visit early in the Carter Administration. That earlier visit was highlighted by Trudeau's address to a joint session of Congress, a speech that was roundly praised by Canadians and Americans alike. Trudeau's remark works on two levels. First, it violates the spirit of formality suggested by the occasion. In doing so, it takes advantage of the moment to make a statement that is reported as idiosyncratic and dramatic.[5] The tension that the scene creates is consistent with the form of the popular news media. Dramatic irony lends its weight to this incident. Edelman's notion of political symbology is useful here:

> Political opposition frequently rallies around a competing metaphorical definition . . . to speak and write in fresh unconventional terms while jargon swirls about one . . . is to state definitively that one is not buying accepted values and not docilely conforming to authority.(pp. 72–73)[6]

Second, the setting in which the metaphor is used is poignant for the politically oriented foreign policy audience; for the cabinet represents the focal point of foreign policy for the American press. And by virtue of the rules of the setting, the formality of the guest being escorted away from a high-level White House meeting with the cabinet in attendance, Trudeau upstaged the Americans' access to the press and their definition of what has transpired in the White House meeting.

This is a very unusual bit of foreign policy news coverage. Its implications for policy depend on the interpretation of the propriety of Trudeau's behavior in this setting as well as his association with the larger issue, the peace mission itself. Implications range from perceptions of the incident as a fit of pique, constituting an insult to the American head of state, on one hand, to admirable, inventive media strategy for rallying support for an important international cause, on the other.

DOMESTIC CEREMONIES VERSUS
INTERNATIONAL ACCOUNTABILITY

On Being There: The Role of Audience Experience
in Suppressing Elite Consensus

Occasionally, Americans are represented in the news as having access to alternative sources of information about foreign affairs, including their own experience with specific policy issues. In those cases in which the audience is shown to have personal experience informing them about international policy, the influence of the elite policymaker's mass-mediated appeals may be limited or even rejected altogether.[7]

Public priorities, attitudes, and responses relating to foreign policy can be influenced by the media. Issues can be raised by news media in ways that are independent of foreign policy power centers.[8] In other words, the media portrayals of citizen experience can counter the often-cited elite domination of policy related experience in news coverage. One news story of this type deals with the transportation of nuclear waste across the Canadian/American border. The report is based in a narrative that dwells on democracy as it resides in the discourse of the traditional American town meeting.

Anchor: One of the nation's oldest democratic traditions is being used tonight to make policy about one of the world's newest problems; nuclear waste. Not just where to put it, but how to get it from here to there. Marlene Sanders reports tonight that of 12 Vermont towns voting, 10 have so far said that on its way there they don't want it here.

Reporter: It's an American institution, the town meeting, and here in Vermont, small town residents are worried about a problem from across the border.

Citizen: Well, the voters brought before the town meeting this article which would restrict and regulate the transportation of high-level radioactive material.

Reporter: They're trying to decide what to do about truck loads of nuclear wastes from a reactor in Ontario, Canada, that goes through their town on its way to a reprocessing plant in South Carolina carrying a deadly cargo that some fear could spread radiation here in an accident.

Citizen #2: We would have to just evacuate our town, essentially. A mile radius around, that's quite a distance.

Citizen #3: I think if you people are so concerned about regulating nuclear shipments, you should also be very concerned about regulating many, many of the hazardous shipments that have gone over the highway including drunk drivers.

Citizen #4: If we have to do it on a local level, even if it's only on the symbolic level, I think you have to make this gesture.

Citizen #5: All those in favor of the passage of this article. . . .

Reporter: What passed is a rule regulating shipments so strictly that it effectively bans them from the area. Such votes, like the one here in Thetford, have not stopped trucks in the past, and it raised complicated legal questions. In fact, state officials here in Vermont are saying the bans are not legally enforceable. Elsewhere, Michigan has already prohibited Canada's nuclear waste from crossing its bridges. And New York has closed its routes as well. In all, 127 cities have made it nearly impossible for the waste to come their way. If other towns in Vermont vote the way they did in Thetford, nuclear wastes from Canada may be stopped.

But by the mid-1980s, the problem will be even closer to home when plants here run out of storage space for their nuclear waste. The problem of where that can be shipped if the public protests will probably have to be settled in courts. Marlene Sanders, CBS News. (CBS 3/1/83, 2:20)

This story presents grass-roots foreign policy processes. For the politically active viewer, this is policy in the incubation stage. There is the likelihood that this issue will become a major one between Canada and the United States requiring interested parties to engage in long-term planning if public communication efforts are to influence policy. And this particular story could be useful to the long-range planning of the specialist. The construction of the story is deceptively simple. Contained within it is the underlying assumption that Canada will be put in conflict with the United States with regard to the disposal of nuclear waste in the future. The story is told under the threat of "problems from across the border"; it is cast in a defensive tone. There is no Canadian spokesperson whatsoever. What is said here is secondary to the presentational form. That is, the tradition, ritual of the democratic town meeting serves as a defense against outside threats. The oppositions that are set up here (given the reporter's predictive claim that the decision will not likely stand up to the larger legal system) are grassroots, anti-Canadian attitudes challenging state and federal law. The incubation, that is likely to appeal to viewers oriented toward foreign policy, is the potential for local antagonism toward Canada with regard to this issue and the inability of the legal system to provide a reasonable response. *Policy* is here defined as symbolic action (the town meeting), but the power of that action, although not great in a legal sense, is symbolically formidable in that it reflects a tradition of discourse that has the potential to *expand* its influence across the policymaking bureaucracy.

Domestic Elections as a Stage for Foreign Policy Discourse

Elections are considered to be the major forum in which the public has the opportunity to make its opinion about foreign policy known. The assumption is that the relationships, whatever they are, between the public and the foreign policy elite are most visible in the domestic election coverage that includes the presentation of foreign affairs issues.[9] Of special interest is the coverage of Canadian and U.S. elections and the foreign policy dimensions that are revealed in such coverage.

The tendency for the news to combine foreign affairs with domestic elections is obvious in excerpts from this news story:

> Reporter: Canadians are about to career sharply to the right towards Ronald Reagan's Washington. They're about to kick out the liberal party which has ruled almost uninterruptedly for the last half-century and bring in the conservatives led by Brian Mulroney whose call has been staggering in its simplicity.
>
> Mulroney: This election is about change. . . .
>
> Reporter: There shall be a change on the 4th of September. Canada, as it does in most things, follows the American trends, and Mulroney follows the Reagan trend.
>
> Reporter: This is one election which is not causing jitters in Washington. Whatever happens, Canada will continue to be our good neighbor to the north, steady, safe, and reliable. Canada's Camelot reawakens only with the fleeting appearances of Pierre Elliot Trudeau.
>
> Moredecai Richler: No, it won't be the same. I mean, Trudeau was a man of true international stature. Mulroney's a slick local politician.
>
> Reporter: Personalities aside, with a Reagan in Washington and a Mulroney in Ottawa, North America will be a conservative continent wall-to-wall for the first time in more than 25 years. Bob Simon, CBS News, Ottawa. (CBS 9/3/84, 3:40)

In the context of the total news sample, this story takes on an ironic import. If a nonpolitically oriented viewer used the network news as his or her sole source for understanding Canadian affairs, the person would see several contradictions. This story depicts Canada as predictable and safe. But the total news sample, as an unfolding text, has suggested that Canada is a threat. There are, after all, Canadian citizens protesting the American Cruise missile, Canadian plans for continuing to transport their nuclear wastes through our various states, the menace of foreign-speaking criminals invading Florida, and Canadian proposals to fight acid rain at the expense of America's economic health.

The assumptions in this particular news story about Canada's passivity and neutrality will have to be weighed carefully by the policymaker. Do they accurately reflect the public response to Canada? Judgments of this type are best informed by an appreciation of the form of news treatment of Canada over time, and the contexts in which a particular story is placed.

WHEN ELITES COLLIDE: NEWS RESPONSES TO POLICYMAKERS IN DISARRAY

Typically, elite government officials are in agreement about foreign affairs matters but tend to disagree more on domestic issues. If they do disagree, there is a greater tendency for the media to challenge government policy.

When this situation occurs, alternatives to official policy become possible. Especially significant for this study is the possibility that the *Canadian disaggregative* perspective may emerge as an alternative explanation for a particular issue. The way the media represent that "foreign" perspective, therefore, becomes significant if there is to be a Canadian influence on American policy.

As we see in this chapter, several stages of television news coverage of acid rain reveal instances of profound disagreement on that issue by key U.S. policymakers. When such disagreement occurs, the news media's influence on foreign policy is at its greatest potential to influence public participation in the issue. But the treatment is typically constrained by a narrative style that excludes detailed information about the issues, strategies for public debate or people to contact to voice an opinion. Instead, debate is closed off; the story is wrapped up in a self-contained narrative logic with a tidy ending having the final effect of shutting down political discourse. The demonstration of the principle of conflicting elites is apparent in the following news form:

Reporter: Soon after Mr. Ruckleshouse formulated his plan, according to several sources, budget director Stockman and Interior Secretary Watt convinced Mr. Reagan that the utility companies were right; that the problem was not serious enough to justify spending billions of dollars to reduce sulphur emissions. Sources agree Ruckleshouse's plan is dead at least until next year's election. He refuses even to be interviewed about acid rain. (NBC 11/18/83, 4:20)

In organizing strategies for public political discourse, policymakers are confronted with the question: Do domestic politics take priority over the protection and nurturing of the United State's reputation for adhering to the principles of international law? The question leads us to explore the characteristics of reports of the Jaffe case. The case was presented as a dilemma for the Reagan Administration and required a hard choice between supporting states' rights on one hand, or violating international law, on the other. The drama of the resolution of the case makes a statement about the administration's relative commitment to Canada, specifically and to principles of international law in general. The story was reported in the following way:

Anchor: A case of a Canadian businessman jailed in Florida — Sidney Jaffe, brought a high-level and highly unusual call today for his release. The call to the Florida Parole Board came from secretary of State Shultz. He said that the jailing of Jaffe is hurting Canadian/American relations. Canada claims two U.S. bounty hunters were out-of-bounds when they went to Canada in 1981, abducted Jaffe and brought him back to Florida. Once there, Jaffe was convicted of land sales violations and bond-jumping and sentenced to 35 years in jail. Ever since, according to Shultz, the Canadians have raised this matter in virtually every high-level contact between the two nations. (CBS 7/26/83, :40)

NBC added citizens appeals to its coverage some days later:

Anchor: Florida's Attorney General said today Florida did not want to release convicted land swindler Sidney Jaffe from jail. Jaffe is a Canadian citizen, and his incarceration has become an international incident with the U.S. Secretary of State and the Canadian government pressing for his release. Lisa Myers reports:

Reporter: Sidney Jaffe, former developer, yachtsman, patron of the arts, now a convicted land swindler, is sentenced to 35 years in this Florida prison. The international dispute centers not on Jaffe's guilt or innocence, but on how he was brought from Canada to Florida to stand trial 3 years ago.

Jaffe: I was kidnapped, beaten, had my life threatened, my family's life threatened, and by this method, they returned me to Florida.

Reporter: The Canadian government has demanded Jaffe's release charging that his abduction by bounty-hunters violated international law and made a mockery of its extradition treaty with the United States. Last week the United States government sided with Canada. In a letter to the Florida Parole Commission, Secretary of State Shultz said that Jaffe's parole is in the national interest. But those who claim Jaffe swindled them out of their savings on deals involving this Florida land say it's none of Shultz's business.

Citizen: This man has swindled a lot of people out of money, and Washington is sitting up there. They don't feel it; they don't care. He did something bad; he was found guilty; he was put in jail. I think he should stay there.

Reporter: Two Florida officials who have fought hardest to keep Jaffe in prison said they will continue to oppose parole until Jaffe makes substantial restitution to all his victims.

Florida Official: We don't care really if he pays restitution. If it's that important to Canada we'll accept their check, a check from the United States Treasury, or from Mr. Jaffe.

Reporter: State Attorney Stephen Boyle said Florida doesn't mind standing up to the Federal government. Even if the Parole Commission releases Jaffe, he may not be home free. State Attorney Boyle filed new fraud charges against Jaffe last month, which could mean many more months of legal problems. Lisa Myers, NBC News, Avon Park, Florida. (NBC 8/2/83, 2:10)

The direct involvement of the people interviewed reveals a set of personal--local–legal constraints on foreign policy. The foreign policy actors (Shultz and the Canadian government) are vague in their broad portrayal. The issues that emerge here involve personal justice versus international relations. The news treatment appeals to the viewer's legal knowledge about international treaties and illegal abduction. However, the voices recruited as evidence are primarily those who favor local justice. Canadian spokespersons are absent, with the resulting implication that there was no cost to Canadians other than Jaffe. The level of the language of this story is restricted to the "common-man" appeal of the people interviewed. The abstract language required to put this story into an international–legal context is absent. This story is cast as a tabloid piece. The oppositions that are set up include victim versus victim constructions. Jaffe, as a victim of the Florida state legal system, is set against Florida citizens presented as an organized, politically active, domestic constituency who were victimized by Jaffe's land schemes. The Canadian government, the U.S. federal government, and the Florida State legal machine are the policy combatants in this *intermestic* drama.[10]

The story provides no clear representation of policymakers' opinions through which a viewer so oriented might interpret the issue. That role is usurped by the accessed citizens' voices whose concerns are for individual justice. The elite are not the center of attention in this story. Nor is the treaty violation an apparent issue in this story. The policy-oriented audience, for one, is likely to judge this issue on the basis of its potential for becoming a cause that would confound foreign policy decisionmaking. Repetitions of this news theme (Americans' individual rights being sacrificed for an abstract point of international law, within different news contexts) could emerge as a dominant meaning in domestic politics for an aroused public.

The apparent resolution of the issue appears in a later story.

Anchor: Well, at one point Canada raised the issue at every high-level meeting with Canadian officials. This summer it led to [*sic*] Secretary of State Shultz and Attorney General Smith to take the rare step of asking Florida to free a convict. The issue: Canadian businessman Sidney Jaffe, abducted from Canada in 1981 by U.S. bounty hunters and brought to Florida to face trial on charges of landsales violations. All the pressure to free Jaffe from top Canadian and U.S. officials has failed to convince Florida to release him that is, until now. Jaffe will be paroled October 11, but he will still have to face a local charge of organized fraud. (CBS 10/5/83, :40)

But what is the nature of the resolution? Does the resolution imply that the administration bows to Canada's demands? If so, how is the U.S. recalcitrance regarding the acid rain issue to be explained comparatively on the basis of TV news coverage? Is the "cost" factor that determines U.S.

response to Canadian demands economic or legalistic? Or is it represented in terms of the American diplomatic image in the international community? By considering a range of audience orientations, we have some flexibility in proposing implications of this discourse of policy resolution. For the pro-Canadian activist orientation the administration is seen to have capitulated to Canadian pressures to release Jaffe in accordance with international law. For American viewers uninformed about the issue, the feds have muscled the state of Florida and her citizens in favor of Canada.

ACID RAIN[11]

During 1983–1984, the acid rain issue festered in the wounds of already troubled Canadian/American relations.[12] During this 2-year period, the acid rain issue began to take on a sinister confrontational tone that continued to escalate.[13] Contributing to the furor were the comments by some Canadians charging that Canada's sense of outrage over U.S. acid rain policy may be hypocritical.[14]

More than any other issue, including cruise missiles and free trade, acid rain dominated television news coverage of Canada for the period. Ten stories from the 1983–1984 period dealt with acid rain. Seven of them are briefly summarized here as a demonstration of the way the method of news analysis was applied; as an index to the range of appeals and language constructions typical of TV news, and to illustrate the kind of discourse used by those who represent Canadian/American relations.

In 1981, in Geneva, Switzerland, 32 European nations, Canada, the United States, and the European Economic Community signed the Convention on Long Range Transboundary Air Pollution also known as the "Acid Rain Convention." This international community of concerned nations constitutes a significant culture in this debate. Many of the nations who signed the convention have come to support the benefits of acid rain abatement, and by July 1985, 21 of them had agreed to cut their sulphur emissions by 30% no later than 1993. The United States has not signed that particular agreement. This analysis tries to understand the nature of the press discourse about acid rain that might have influenced America's acid rain policy.[15]

The main arguments associated with the acid rain issue that the press could have engaged in its coverage include:

1. Canada's geography (composed of acidic granite bedrock with very little natural buffering protection from acid rain) and industry

(high dependency on forest product revenues) compared to that of the United States are especially vulnerable to acid deposition.

2. Although both countries are responsible for transborder acid deposition, the United States is responsible for 50% of Canada's deposition and that is dispersed over a large geographic area with comparatively serious environmental effects. Canada, meanwhile, contributes to approximately 20% of U.S. acid deposition and the effects of that pollution are restricted to the Northeastern section of the United States.[16]

3. American industry proposes to respond to the threat after significant proof of "causation" is established through further tests, and then if "causation" is proved, the industry will respond by making cleaner, less polluting plants as it replaces older, sulfur-coal-burning facilities. Environmentalists argue for more stringent measures and policies that respond more quickly to what they believe are demonstrated cases of environmental damage. The main point of contention between American industry and international environmentalists is whether or not there is sufficient proof that U.S. coal-fired industries are responsible for acid rain and, if so, how to balance the costs of environmental damage against the costs, to American industry, of abatement of acid deposition.[17]

4. Canada has been accused by pro-U.S. business lobbyists of launching an aggressive "propaganda" media campaign to increase awareness of the acid rain issue in the United States.[18]

NBC 1/2/83, 3:20. The American government, as represented in a Reagan administration-industry coalition, is confronted by the news, which attributes acid rain to American industry. The lack of consensus among the American policy elite on the acid rain issue is evident in the Congressional disagreement over the proposed Mitchell–Stafford amendment recommending that American industries sharply reduce their acid rain emissions. Canadian public opinion is clearly represented, and its appeals are pro-environmental, not pro-Canadian per se. The Reagan Administration appeals are for economic protection of the nation's industries. All of the actors recruited for this news story are cast in these two camps. Ambassador Allan Gotlieb says, "I don't think there is any issue of greater concern to Canadians than acid rain." The American ambassador to Canada, Mr. Robinson, bases his appeals in the conservative vision of industry. An American industry spokesperson uses threatening language and fear appeals suggesting that the costs of reducing acid rain will ultimately be born by the consumers. Dr. Dillon, a Canadian environmental researcher, appeals to the public's sense of environmental ethics. The news voices here are organized in a way that portrays the Reagan Administration's acid rain policy as defensive, motivated by domestic politics, protectionist, and insensitive to environmental concerns. A favorable interpretation of the Canadian position on the acid rain issue is encouraged. The combined appeal is to an international constituency whose shared sense of environmental propriety is threatened by the administration's policy. The news defines the problem as a threat to Canadian/American relations. There is no indication of a U.S. public response, but the concern for the Canadian public opinion response to U.S. policy is apparent throughout the story. Reagan is presented (via old news clips) as trying to placate the Canadians. The news here confronts U.S. government policy. The Canadian environmental activist ideology with regard to the acid rain issue emerges as the dominant level of appeal through which the news organizes its discourse. This particular story serves as one likely example of the disjunctive coorientation for administration policymakers. For here is unexpected opposition to administration policy. The news has apparently organized its appeals in the absence of a clear administration consensus on the acid rain issue.

The environmentalist voices use appeals to individual conscience, as exemplified in the statements of Dr. Dillon. Ambassador Gotlieb appeals to our sense of international community and ideal social order, whereas the Reagan Administration appeals tend to be the community guardian and authoritarian types.

CBS 6/29/83, 1:10. The news again confronts the Reagan Administration's acid rain policy. The administration's position is articulated by the U.S. government elite. Scientist Calvert of The National Academy of Science concludes that because "we've answered the question of effects, action (against acid rain) can be taken." The Environmental Protection Agency (EPA) versus scientist is set up as a confrontation. The language of the news drives the confrontation. First, the news verifies the scientific conclusion as "official." Then, acting EPA Director Ruckleshouse's admonition that the "situation requires careful study" is challenged. This story supports Canada's long-term position that Reagan is stalling. Its presentation of domestic scientific support serves as verification of the causation argument; that American industry causes acid rain, which damages the Canadian environment. This interpretation is shown to be officially accepted by domestic experts. The news predicts conflicting reactions between industry and a coalition of scientists and environmentalists. Ruckleshouse is shown making a public opinion appeal: they must "sort through [the scientific data] to decide what public interest dictates." The news story indicts the motives of Ruckleshouse and the EPA by associating his appeals with the position of industry. The language of the report is encouraging for transnational collaboration among environmentalists in Canada and the

United States in their efforts to reduce acid rain. The news sets up and predicts the confrontation by using pugilistic and "stormy weather" metaphors.

The less-than-flattering portrayal of the government's stock, defensive, self-serving response is a prediction of how the United States will respond to environmental appeals. Cues are given to the environmentalists for organizing their rhetorical strategies. Together, the appeals in this particular news story have the potential to invite a collective political response from those publics who are concerned about acid rain.

ABC 8/23/83, 0:10. Here, the United States appears to accept the causation thesis, but nevertheless fails to take action. This story gives the impression that the administration, while stalling, is putting on a face of action, a gloss of cooperation. This story is delivered only through the voice of the news anchor. There is no field reporter's video evidence and commentary. Compared with the CBS story just reviewed, the United States appears to have changed its attitude. But viewed through the definition of the administration as stalling, as set up in previous reports of the issue by this and other networks, the U.S. agreement for government research simply feigns policy activity. It offers research as a token action; substituting the ceremony of domestic bureaucratic activity for international policy change.

NBC 10/16/83, 2:50. This story shows Canada's continuing pressure on the United States about the acid rain issue and the public significance of the conflict over acid rain among the administration elite. A crack in the administration's diplomatic facade is revealed. The press, as if sensing this fracture, moves in with untypically detailed argument against the administration's acid rain policy. The news confronts the administration, and berates the conflicting agency spokespersons. The viewer is shown Secretary of state George Schultz visiting Halifax and walking into an apparently solid Canadian citizen's public demonstration against U.S. acid rain policy. Schultz's dilemma is compounded by the earlier presentation of the disagreement over this issue at home between his administration colleagues and the scientific community. Cut-away shots and reporter's words pointing out a Soviet boat in the Halifax harbor provide an ironic reminder of Canada's autonomy; Canada's international relations are not necessarily a mirror image of the United States'. Here, the news is uncharacteristically detailed in its presentation of U.S. interagency conflict over acid rain. The United States is shown to be late in delivering to Canada its promised control program. The news develops the tardiness metaphor into a recurring motif complete with puns. Meanwhile, Canadian Environmental Minister Charles Caccia, says he has a plan he wants Schultz to take to Washington.

The administration is shown to be blind to the information about interagency conflict that is disclosed by this reportage. The piece is potentially invitational for detractors of the administration's policy regarding the acid rain issue.

The causation argument, that American industrial pollution is directly linked to the production of acid rain, is accepted in this coverage. The perception that the administration's environmental image is poor is reinforced. The news concludes that acid rain comes from the United States; that Canadians are upset, and as a result, the reporter tells us, that the U.S. image is suffering: "Americans are losing friends while Canadians are losing thousands of dollars." Again, Canadians are portrayed as victims of American policy.

The news recruits a host of Canadian spokespersons by attribution ("Canadian officials," "Canadians say," "Senior Canadian diplomats," "another Canadian diplomat") in order to support the argument. Clearly, Canadian public opinion is invoked here: "Nothing in recent history has troubled them more than the administration's inaction on acid rain." The administration's position is presented derisively through David Stockman's simplistic observation that curbing acid rain "would cost Americans $6–10,000 to save each pound of Canadian fish." The implications for politically active viewers are that interagency agreement must be achieved and progress demonstrated if Canadian pressure is to be alleviated. Here, nationalism is rejected as a logical explanation for the United States' failure to act.

Again, the news offers predictions. It predicts that the administration will try to buy time, and that the environmental image of the United States and of the administration, in particular, will continue to suffer if the policy is not confronted.

ABC 2/22/84, :20. This report, delivered exclusively by the news anchor with only a static graphic over his shoulder, is described as a "scientific note." The report confronts the myth of positive relations between Canada and the United States by suggesting that the United States, while stalling in its acid rain clean-up, is violating international law; violating a treaty. The story suggests that the controversy is incorrectly positioned as a domestic political issue, but is instead an issue of law between the two countries, that is, the violation of an international treaty. This news interpretation is consistent with and gains force from a politically oriented viewer's awareness of Canada's historical frustration with the tendency of U.S. domestic politics to confound and forestall the conclusion of treaties between the two countries.

CBS 2/22/84, :10. This news item is also treated as a scientific note. In this case, acid rain is considered as one of several environmental issues.

But here the tone confronts and ridicules the environmentalists' position on acid rain. This ridicule emerges in the comparison of acid rain described by some as "more of a threat (to the environment) than we thought" (attributed to Canadians) with recent National Academy of Science findings that aerosol sprays are "less of a threat to the ozone layer than we thought." The implication is that Canadian environmentalists are alarmist, irrational, and need to consider the long view. Rhetorically, the news calls for historical proofs from the acid rain activists. This is consistent with the Reagan Administration position that has been heretofore challenged in the news sample. The story also reveals the positivist orientation of the news with its ongoing ceremony of uncritically presenting scientific explanations of political issues as fact. This example demonstrates one way in which the news engages in the politics of scientific discourse. But clearly, the news uses the scientific evidence in ways that best serve its rhetorical intent. Compare this story with CBS 6/29/83 (reviewed earlier) in which a different report from this agency, the National Academy of Science, was used to construct an argument *against* the administration's acid rain policy. Both arguments are from the same TV network.

The tone of this story shows that the ideological position of the news can result from apparently opportunistic constructions. The story also demonstrates how the news can be inconsistent (both within and among networks) in its long-term coverage of the same issue. Acid rain is treated somewhat dismissively in a context of findings that debunk the notion of ozone depletion by aerosols. The efficacy of the news construction as determined by news conventions apparently takes precedence over concerns for logical and consistent political discourse.

NBC 6/20/84, 2:00.   This story is comparatively unusual for the acid rain coverage because it creates the impression that the government has achieved consensus on one aspect of the acid rain issue. The story is based on a Congressional report on acid rain. The political posture of the report ("do nothing about acid rain until more studies have been completed") is not confronted. The suggestion here is that the Canadians' claims of environmental damage and their call for immediate action are questionable in the face of this Congressional report. The Reagan policy of waiting is an acceptable option in this report.

The reporter views the claims: Acid rain may be the cause of environmental damage; industry may be to blame. Dollar costs of acid rain damage now total $6 billion. Canada claims to be suffering. . . . Canada says the risks outweigh the costs. . . . Canada says "we can't wait." The connection between this story and the previous one reveals the progress of bureaucratic public discourse, for here is the ritual of the Congressional report following the scientific report. The news coverage reveals political backfilling as a form of official legitimation of administration policy. The claim that environmental protection costs jobs is at the heart of the administration rhetoric here and the news recruits voices to support that contention. One industry spokesman's appeal (Carl Bagge, Natl. Coal Assn.) is typical; "you've got to balance costs."

When viewed with the previous story, this report suggests that the networks have made an ideological shift from challenging the administration's position on acid rain toward accepting it. The scientific report seems to have generated a consensus about acid rain among policymakers, and in the face of that consensus the news confrontation of administration policy subsides. This analysis encourages the conclusion that the news is organized to play a story for its rhetorical, dramatic worth, even if those constructions are not consistent with earlier political interpretations. Over the long haul, such patterns of reporting tend to confirm the charge in previous research that TV news is blind to history in general. Here it apparently ignores its own past interpretations of the acid rain issue for Canadian/American affairs.[19]

METAMEDIA: THE CANADIAN NATIONAL FILM BOARD DOCUMENTARIES

On February 25, 1983, three documentaries produced by The National Film Board (NFB) of Canada were officially labeled "propaganda" by the U.S. Justice Department. Two of the films were about acid rain, and the third, nominated for an Academy Award, dealt with the threat of nuclear weapons. The Justice Department ruling required that the documentaries carry a disclaimer at each showing in the United States.

Besides the obvious connection to the acid rain controversy, the network coverage of the NFB issue illustrates the way news definitions and treatments of a variety of Canadian/American issues tend to become infused with and informed by each other. This happens in ways that have the appearance of logic, accuracy, and closure. The selective way the news ties together the loose ends of a variety of Canadian/American affairs has implications for the organization of the agenda of public political discourse about acid rain.

All four of the NFB news stories were analyzed. The major characteristics of the four NFB news stories are presented here for illustrative purposes.

ABC 2/25/83, 2:20. The report begins with an unusual first-person appeal by the news anchor. It discloses, at the outset, the intensity of the anti-administration tone. Anchorman Frank Reynolds appeals to our sense of federal bureaucratic propriety by summarizing the apparent violation of the special relationship between Canada and the United States:

> It may come as a surprise to you to learn that the Justice Department is in the business of reviewing films. And that all three films made in Canada, of all places, have been disapproved by the critics at Justice who have declared them to be political propaganda and have decided that in this country people who watch the films must be told their government does not like them. Now you probably think I made up all of this, but it's true. Here's a report from Roger Peterson.

The news argument put forward is that the Justice Department has insulted the American tradition of free speech. What's more, it has done so in a way that threatens international relations. In short, the news argues that this ruling has diplomatic implications and that assumptions about U.S./Canadian friendship have been violated by this policy. The appeals selected and orchestrated to construct this argument are those that encourage political discourse and invite viewer involvement; the appeals are to individual conscience and to an ideal social order. Historical proofs are used as part of the news construction to support the claim. Senator Kennedy, for example, is shown suggesting that the Justice Department is engaging in bookburning and McCarthyisms. The recruited voices are used to build a sense of Canadian/American coalition that is pro-environmental and standing strong for the western tradition of freedom of speech. Helen Caldicott and Allan Gotlieb along with Senator Kennedy are among the prominent voices. Gotlieb, appealing to the government's respect for democratic discourse, asks that the order be repealed. He assures us, that "propaganda, in a democratic society, isn't a film about topical issues." Meanwhile, nuclear activist Helen Caldicott contends that democracy requires that such films be made and shown.

Canada emerges as being sympathetic to the news definition of Americans' rights to freedom of speech. Meanwhile, Canada-as-victim emerges as a theme. The power of the news to orchestrate international discourse about a particular policy is apparently confirmed.

This story includes interagency responses to the Justice Department's policy and demonstrates further how one agency's public misfortunes can be used by another for apparent public opinion advantage. Such is the nature of the use of the press by policymakers. What appears to be operating here in the TV news version of the issue, is that the Department of Justice is suffering the consequences of the policy boomerang effect that occurs when an agency forfeits control of a particular policy through the unexpected influences of public discourse. In this case, television news has preempted the definition and articulation of that policy. This is, in terms of this study, an example of *disjunction.* The Department of Justice is portrayed as remaining silent, as if having assessed the political power of the news discourse, it has decided to retreat in order to avoid further damage to its credibility.[20]

The news attributes special significance to the issue by announcing that it "will be explored further tonight on *Nightline,*" that network's late-night news analysis program.

NBC 2/25/83, 1:50. The Canadian government is shown aggressively challenging the Justice Department ruling. Again, Ambassador Gotlieb supports the shared democratic traditions of Canada and the United States: "We're a democracy; you're a democracy, we don't understand (this)." Caldicott appeals to the special relationship "Canada is an ally, this can't be propaganda." Both Gotlieb and Caldicott, in appealing to shared traditions rather than engaging in confrontational rhetoric against the American state, are aligned with the citizens in a state-versus-citizens' rights drama that has been set up by the reports. The news treatment has them taking their places in the crowd of Americans who appear to be offended by the state's threat to freedom of speech.

In contrast, J. Domville, from the Canadian National Film Board, seems secure in his conclusion that the Justice Department dictum "is a futile gesture." And Canadian Communication Minister Francis Fox predicts the issue "will be an embarrassment for the government." Meanwhile, Vermont Senator Stafford and Massachusetts Senator Kennedy are presented as unyielding opponents of the Justice Department ruling. Amidst all of this discourse, there are many references to Canadian/American friendship and the long tradition of that friendship.

This story is typical of the previous NFB issue coverage in that an extraordinary number of Canadian spokespersons are recruited to support the news interpretation. Ambassador Gotlieb's words suggest that the Department of Justice ruling is linked to the Reagan Administration's acid rain policy. The Ambassador remarks: "Acid rain from the U.S. is a view not fully accepted by the Reagan Administration."

The litany of appeals by U.S. government agencies and members of the policy elite is the display of consequence. For their appeals reflect attempts to disassociate themselves in the public's eye from the Justice Department's ruling. This story has the potential to serve as an invitation for U.S. policy elites to collide, and for select Canadian and American elites and attentive publics to join together in opposition to this policy.

Significantly, the language issuing from the administration's representatives does not recognize the NFB dilemma as an international issue; it frames it domestically. The news appears to recruit voices from Canadian and American government spokespersons in a way that favors the Canadian political position with regard to the environmental issues covered in the films. Closer analysis, however, reveals that these voices were recruited primarily in order to support a definite anti-governmental posture, with the collective news narratives taking the role of defender of the principles of freedom of speech and recruiting the Canadians to voice support for the shared democratic traditions of freedom of expression that were apparently violated by the Justice Department ruling. One interpretation is that the news uses the Canadian voices as proofs to enhance its argument and to provide the dramatic tension for the news rhetoric about values that are a significant part of the traditional ideals for the political function and ethos of western journalism. In short, the main effect of the news coverage of this issue for those viewers who are not politically involved with the issue covered may be primarily to enhance the credibility and authority of the news sources.[21]

Such an interpretation is encouraged by the likelihood that for a general audience orientation, the details of the acid rain issue are obscured in this news coverage. No alternatives to policy are provided; no strategies are proposed for sustaining the Canadian/American coalition that is assembled by the recruitment of voices for the story.[22]

CBS 2/24/83, :20. Several dimensions of this particular story are significant. First, the Justice Department serves as a test case, a first target, for the administration's policy. Its behavior here reflects the classic trial balloon phenomenon associated with bureaucratic strategy; while one agency tests the public response to policy, other agencies are watching. The apparent misfortune of the Justice Department, in this instance occasioned by a vigorous press, does not necessarily evoke sympathy from competing government agencies, especially those that may be actively arguing for different foreign policy strategies. The viewer is appealed to as a media consumer whose freedom of choice is threatened by the censorship implied in the Justice Department ruling. The news confronts the government by revealing how this policy contradicts an American ritual of film legitimacy, namely the Academy Awards for film excellence. One of the Canadian films involved has been nominated for an Oscar. The Justice Department ruling collides with both the ritual of the Academy Awards and the myth of freedom of speech in America, and ironically, the previous legitimation of the acid rain film by another government agency, the National Forest and Wildlife Service, which had given the film an award for excellence. The irony is compounded in the image of the Justice Department attacking one of the institutions (freedom of expression) it is assumed to be responsible for protecting. The Justice Department is charged with having engaged in an ad hoc policy because no consultation or forewarning for this policy is made apparent. This implies that the ritual of public discourse, as represented in the airing of public opinion or through due process by elected representatives of the public, has been short-circuited. There is no indication of how the policy evolved. The implicit charge is that the Justice Department is here serving as an irrational, knee-jerk advocate of the administration's nationalistic acid rain policy toward Canada. The news exacerbates the confrontation of the people versus the government.

There seems to be a contagion-effect at work for this particular issue involving all three networks. The level of anti-government discourse heightens with each day's coverage. It is as if an incubation process is operating in the informal professional–collegial channels among the television journalists legitimating the anti-governmental news constructions.

CBS 2/25/83, 2:10. This story focuses more on the Justice Department's critical acumen than its threat to free speech.

Senators and Capitol Hill staffers are set against the Department of Justice. The reporter labels the Justice Department as "petty and just plain wrong." The news, offering no specific source for these labels, is speaking with its most confrontational voice in the total television news sample. The viewer is presented with a Canadian/American coalition poised against the Department of Justice.

By saying that "environmentalists are thrilled with the attention brought on by the controversy," the reporter reveals an implicit journalistic assumption; that news coverage influences policy, or at least plays to those who are engaged in attempts to influence policy. The comment is noteworthy, for it is inherently reflexive; it is a subjective claim, unverified by the presentation of supporting evidence. It provides a glimpse of the reporter from behind the conventional journalistic mask of objectivity revealing his assumptions about the political dimensions of the communications encounters in which journalists and audience are engaged.[23] It is an aside in the formality of news conventions that allows us to recognize how the normally hidden, implicit theories drive journalists' political constructions.

The film clips from the documentaries in question play in the background while the reporter views the Justice Department's policy.[24] The definition of propaganda offered by "Justice" (the abbreviated form "Justice" is used in the news language and is one of many examples reflecting TV journalists' enculturation to the Washington bureaucracy by comfortably adopting their idioms) is confronted by selected evidence. The recruited voices here include Helen Caldicott, who, in one of the documentary excerpts, discusses the effects of nuclear fallout. Meanwhile, the reporter reminds us that the Justice Department has remained silent since their ruling. Democratic Senator George Mitchell of Maine suggests collusion between the Department of Justice and the Reagan Administration. He concludes that the ruling "is consistent with Reagan policy" and thereby provides yet another claim that there is a strategic connection between the Justice Department ruling and the administration's acid rain policy. Rhetorically, the construction raises questions about the propriety of using the Justice Department for purposes of supporting administration policy. Canada's Minister of the Environment, John Roberts, appeals to Americans' sense of freedom: "Americans are being insulted by this." This is followed by Secretary of State Schultz's confused, inarticulate bureaucratise, which suggests that there is no government consensus about the policy. Schultz says: "We must stand for principles of freedom of expression, but how to define principles of freedom of speech is not clear in this case."

Finally, after the reporter tells us that "the Justice Department refused TV interview requests," the voice of the Department of Justice is heard. Its introduction, as a response to the "storm of protest" sets it up for ridicule: "Our action should not be construed as censorship or intimidation." The Justice Department is appealing to the public to reject the news definition of its policy. In view of the consistency among networks in their coverage of this issue, rejection of the news definition seems unlikely. Besides, the strained, formalized bureaucratic language used by both Secretary of State Schultz and the Justice Department in their press statement is typical of administrative language that encourages ridicule rather than compliance or sympathy on the part of an aroused public political constituency.[25]

The news emerges as an independent voice here. This sequence of network stories serves as an example of how the news can symbolically isolate and negatively define a nondiscursive governmental agency, in this case the Department of Justice. This is an instance of the networks, together, circling the wagons in defense of an ideal; the tradition of western journalism as defender of free speech. The coverage also serves as a demonstration of the way in which government bureaucrats can observe and participate in mass mediated interagency blood-letting in order to enhance their own credibility as policymakers. The news provides the stage and the stage director. The bureaucrats, government elite, and selected Canadians are at once the actors in the drama and the selected rhetorical elements used to construct the arguments of the news stories. Occasionally, certain policies are reactive for the broad range of news audience orientations outlined earlier in this study. This is one of those occasions. Given the appropriate mix of news availability, interagency consensus (or lack thereof, as in this case), international climate, the news networks do engage in coordinated responses to policy. This policy was politicized through the news coverage which here constructs a consensual image of mutual outrage on the part of United States and Canadian political elite.

These particular national reports are guided by the unusually willing-hands of the news producers. For here we have the selective presentation of administration opponents, statements supporting environmentalists and a Justice Department in apparent retreat from the media blitz.

In the acid rain coverage, the voices that specifically represent the Reagan Administration make appeals that tend to reinforce existing political beliefs as they have been defined by pro-American policies. The basis of these administration (as distinct from news reporter) appeals is that the appropriate action for audiences is to support the administration policies suggested to be in their best interests. In the context of the acid rain issue, this translates into support for the pro-industry position. The policy rationale behind the appeals is that every American's interest is invested figuratively and literally in the success of American industry. Canadian interests, as represented in appeals supporting environmental action are, at best, treated as secondary to American interests.

The news assembles appeals through combined voices and through its reportorial commentary, initially challenging the administration's nationalistic orientation. On the surface, this coverage appears to deny the frequent charge in international news research suggesting that American news is inherently nationalistic; following and confirming America's foreign policy rather than providing a forum in which questions are raised that negotiate or confront America's policies. This case suggests that the provision of a forum in which policy is challenged is the exception rather than the rule in the news; and when such constructions do occur, they are more the result of the business of constructing drama than of systematic, logical, and consistent strategies of political inquiry about particular issues. The news is more the product of strategies that are invested with dramatic opportunism than with calculated persuasive campaigns espousing a particular ideology. When the news embraces nationalism, it assumes that posture more for the purposes of achieving its routinized communication objectives than to exercise patriotic zeal.[26] The main agenda of the news and the basis for its rhetorical urgency is the construction of appropriate news form. Television news interprets policy, however it must, within a broad range of normative acceptability to achieve that end, which gives priority to the logic of its drama and organizes appeals accordingly. Appeals are located within dramatic contexts, and dramatic treatments lend the appeals their particular political potential.

Across networks, the news did an about face on the acid rain issue after the presentation of organized scientific reports and government consensus about those reports, shifting from a pro-Canadian-environmental posture to apparent support for the Reagan Administration's policy position. Later, in response to the censuring of the NFB films, the news networks together aggressively confronted the Justice Department for a ruling that the news suggested was an extension of the Reagan Administration's acid rain policy. It seized these dramatic opportunities even at the expense of twice contradicting the logic of its earlier coverage of the acid rain issue. Such examples suggest that the news as a discursive voice has the tendency to operate beyond international policy issues. That is, it covers foreign affairs issues not to negotiate or confront those issues per se, but uses them to make appeals to the public in order to create dramas that will continue to attract audiences to its ongoing narratives. Recognizing this pattern, we are left with the task of trying to predict how these appeals, in their final form, regardless of their role in the agenda of the news organizations, are used by audiences in understanding and becoming involved in Canadian/American relations.

The charge by U.S. pro-industry spokespersons that Canada was conducting an anti-acid rain propaganda campaign in the United States is weakened considerably when we realize the extent to which TV news domesticates Canadian voices to comply with its rheortical forms.

SUMMARY

Television news is distinguished by several characteristics. These are listed here.

1. Television news strains toward a popular narrative form that substitutes the news reporters' views and visual images in place of foreign policy processes, especially details from the Canadian perspective.
2. Television news uses pathos; emotional appeals as a primary, recurring formal element.
3. The American policymakers represented in television news are supported by recruited voices. There are "common man" witnesses representing the public at large to whom appeals are directed and from whom appeals issue forth in common language. The shape of public opinion and the appeals that are made to publics are non-inviting in terms of political action and the appeals that do emerge are more likely to come from the selective TV constructions of narrative than from the words of the policy makers themselves.
4. Television news tends to subordinate political discourse to its languages of presentational form; familiarizes rather than defamiliarizes, and in so doing routinizes and domesticates international affairs.

In television news, there is a kind of narrative inertia, a built-in memory of the news heritage from which it springs, a strain toward story-telling that celebrates omniscient narration while discouraging audience participation. Active response is more likely to be dependent on the interpretive skills and sensitivity to exposition brought to the text by the audience, if such a response is to occur at all. The tendency of the news to generate popular narrative forms is so prevalent that it routinely spilled over the analytical frames used in this study. More significantly, the endless repetitions of this tendency work to repress details of Canadian/American relations.

The pervasiveness of appeals to and invocations of the public suggests that public opinion, already identified in the research as a problematic concept, requires much greater refinement as a communication variable if we are to understand how meaning in public discourse is translated into policy. The findings for television news vary somewhat from past research showing that there is the tendency for television networks to be consonant in favoring a pronationalistic viewpoint in foreign news reporting. The networks do confront government policy over the short run in dramatistic if not in politically significant ways.

Hallin and Mancini's comparative study of TV news convincingly shows how the narrative conventions of American TV news serve up "heroes, contest, tests of will," whereas Italian TV news presents ideological debate via abstract political ideas and invites the viewer to participate in kind. On the basis of these examples, I am inclined to agree with their conclusions that political discourse is comparatively restrained in American TV news:

> American TV news is (politically) exclusive . . . in the sense that it presents the interpretation of political events as belonging to a sphere that includes the journalists themselves and other political elites; but does not include the audience. (p. 846)[27]

However, the approach of this study has been to qualify the tendencies of news form to repress or invite public discourse about international relations by concentrating on a politically active audience orientation interacting with news form. The apparent exclusion of the audience in the news reports themselves does not explain away the likelihood that an important audience is using the news in significantly political ways. Further, by framing the analysis within the communication activity of political judgment on the part of the active audience, I have tried to demonstrate how political judgment has the potential to confront news form. It does so by allowing viewers to bring to the news their portable discursive tendencies (including sensitivity to contradiction, the knowledge of the historical and cultural contexts in which international relations are played out, etc.) and thereby use news as one of several information sources that catalyze interpersonal political discourse. The significance of the audience dimension for this interpretation of news function is most dramatically apparent when we realize that such interpersonal political discourse responds to the very absence of news about a particular political issue. One does not have to strain his imagination to conclude that environmental activist coalitions in Canada and the United States increase their public communications efforts as a direct response to the fact that television news covers their favored topics of preoccupation only occasionally and, then, in superficial ways.

NOTES

1. Morley, J. (1988). [Editorial]. *The Nation, 247* (14), 480.
2. For a discussion of the function of predictive news form in another international political context see Barton and Gregg, Op. Cit.
3. Edelman, M. (1977). *Political language: Words that succeed and policies that fail* (p. 123). New York: Academic Press.
4. For a discussion of "oppositional codes" in a news context see Hartley, J. (1982). *Understanding news.* London: Methuen.
5. This example recalls the Formalist critic's notion of defamiliarization or "making strange." "Artistic" speech, according to the Formalists, lifts itself outside the realm of the expected and calls attention to itself. For a discussion of this idea see Lemon, L., Lee, L., & Reis, M. (Eds.). (1965). *Russian Formalist criticism: Four essays.* Lincoln, NE: The University of Nebraska Press.
6. Edelman, 1971, Op. Cit., pp. 72–73. Frye reviewed a similar use of language for political effect in his discussion of "associative monologue." Frye, N. (1963). *The well tempered critic.* Bloomington, IN: The Indiana University Press. (See especially pp. 30–33.)
7. Paletz and Entman, Op. Cit., p. 194.
8. For a discussion of this idea as it applies to newspapers see Commission on Newspapers, Vol. 7. (1981). Ottawa: Canadian Government Publishing Centre.
9. Op. Cit., Soderlund and Wagenberg.
10. This term identifies the policy implications of international relations interacting with domestic affairs. Brewer, T. Op. Cit., pp. 14–15.
11. An earlier version of this acid rain study appears in Barton, R. L. (1988). TV news and the language of acid rain in Canadian–American relations. *Political Communication and Persuasion, 5* (1), 49–65.
12. While acid rain occurs as a result of natural processes (Bollini recorded acid rain generated by the volcano Vesuvius in 1939) acid rain as a manmade pollutant has been recognized since 1852 when it was first studied by Angus Smith in and around Manchester, England. It is a mixture of strong mineral acids, sulfuric, nitric, and in some locations hydrochloric. Acid rain is a problem because it acidifies streams and lakes. The result is a progressive elimination of sensitive species of plant and animals including fish. Pollution by acid rain affecting Canadian/American relations is attributed to the combustion of fossil fuels, chiefly coal and oil, by power plants and industry in the midwestern United States, particularly the Ohio Valley. The subsequent emission of these pollutants through high smokestacks (which allow the polluters to meet local pollution standards) distribute the pollutants

over vast areas with profound effects on the environment especially in Canada and the northeast United States. For further details see Gorham, E. (1982). Acid rain: Questions and answers. In P. S. Gold (Ed.), *Acid rain: A transjurisdictional problem in search of a solution* (pp. 429). Buffalo, NY: The Canadian American Center, State University of New York at Buffalo.

13. In an especially strongly worded letter, Canadian ambassador Allan Gotlieb rebuked Secretary of the Interior Donald Hodel for suggesting that Canada's complaints about U.S.-produced acid rain are a way to sell more electricity, *The Toronto Globe and Mail,* 2/14/87. In response to this particular confrontation the *New York Times* speculated that "Mr. Reagan will no doubt feel the fallout of this exchange when he visits the Canadian Capital April 5 and 6." *The New York Times,* 2/17/87.

14. Canadian author Gwynn commented that "most hypocritical of all, the principal cause of the devastation of Canadian forests is not acid rain, wherever its origin, but the woodcutting and silvaculture practices-or rather, the lack of them-of Canadian lumber companies and governments" (p. 259). Gwynn, *The 49th Paradox,* p. 259.

15. See Rosencranz, J. E. (Ed.). (1988). *International environmental diplomacy.* Cambridge: Cambridge University Press).

16. For a summary of this research see Carroll, J. E. The acid rain issue in Canadian–American relations: A commentary. In J. E. Carroll (Ed.), Op. Cit., pp. 141–146.

17. For a useful discussion of the political dimensions of acid rain see Rosencranz, A. Op. Cit.

18. McMahon, M. S. Balancing the interests: An essay on the Canadian–American acid rain debate. In J. E. Carrol, Op. Cit., pp. 147–171.

19. This interpretation seems especially appropriate if we assume that TV newscasts constitute an ongoing text about policy issues that is layered by reports of each day's political events, and is used selectively by politically oriented viewers, including policymakers. Such audiences tend to systematically survey and organize reports from a range of press forms for information about the public climate as it relates to specific policy issues. See, for example, Davison, W. P., 1976 (Ibid).

20. For a discussion of interagency relations and the use of the media among foreign policy bureaucrats see Stairs, D. (1977–1978). Public opinion and external affairs: Reflections on the domestication of Canadian foreign policy. *International Journal, 33* (1), 128–149.

21. The tension that is created by expectations for journalists to engage in adversarial comment while concurrently meeting the requirements of attracting and holding audiences by way of journalistic form are most frequently discussed under the heading of "news in objectivity." For an enlightened alternative to that approach see Mcquail, D. (1986). From objectivity and back: Competing paradigms for news analysis and a pluralistic alternative. In T. McCormack (Ed.), *News and knowledge* (pp. 1–36). Greenwich, CT: JAI Press.

22. Further support for this interpretation is provided by the lack of attention given this issue by the networks on April 28, 1987 when the supreme court upheld the law (a 45-year-old provision of the *Foreign Agents Registration Act*) on which the Justice Department NFB ruling was based. The court decision was based

specifically on the three NFB films discussed here after the law was challenged by a California state senator. TV journalism offered only a superficial response to this important resolution of the NFB case as if the dramatic worth of the issue had been exhausted in their coverage 4 years earlier. One explanation, from a public discourse perspective, is that the issue had simply outlived its public rhetorical urgency; the larger political context had changed to the extent that this was no longer a significant issue. For a discussion of the historical dimension associated with an active rhetorical situation in public discourse see Bitzer, L. F. (1968). The rhetorical situation. *Philosophy and Rhetoric, 1, 5.*

23. For a discussion of reflexivity in film and video see Ruby, J. (1977). The image mirrored: Reflexivity and the documentary film. *The Journal of the University Film Association 29*(4), 3–11.

24. For a discussion of the documentary as a politically discursive form see Barton, R. L. (1983). Message analysis in international mass communication research: A rhetorical example. In M. Mander (Ed.), *Communications in transition* (pp. 81–102). New York: Praeger.

25. For a discussion of this linguistic phenomenon see Edelman, M. (1985). *The symbolic uses of politics.* Urbana, IL: University of Illinois Press.

26. This is, of course, not to dismiss the likelihood of ideologies, attitudes, and even behaviors being influenced by news constructions. Marxist-oriented media analysts have argued this point endlessly; often in ways that overlook the selective, inventive, idiosyncratic ways that politically motivated people negotiate the news.

27. Allin, D. C., & Mancini, P. (1984). Speaking of the President: Political structure and representational form in U.S. and Italian television news. *Theory and Society 13* (6), 829–850.

Chapter 6

American Cruise Missiles Over Canada: A Comparison of American and International Press Accounts of Canadian Sovereignty

I am the space you desecrate as you pass through.
—Margaret Atwood from "Backdrop
Addresses Cowboy" (p. 51)[1]

HISTORICAL BACKGROUND

The American AGM-86B cruise missile also known as ALCM (air-launched cruise missile) is designed to be launched over the north pole by B-52 bombers. Following the launch, the B-52 is to turn toward home while the missile continues to fly to targets in the USSR. The cruise flies low in order to escape radar detection. This missile is assumed to be very accurate, difficult to identify and destroy. There is some debate about whether the cruise is a first or second strike weapon. Generally, U.S. officials publicly maintain that the function of the cruise is to knock-out communications and command centers as a second-strike weapon. The cruise missile was obviously perceived by the American government as an element in the Strategic Arms Limitation Talks (SALT) discourse. The initial assumption was that the characteristics of this particular weapon would lend force to the American position in the talks without being unduly threatening to the Soviets:

> The United States could acquire a capability to destroy Soviet ICBM silos in a second strike without posing a first-strike threat to the Soviet ICBM force by procuring large numbers of bomber-delivered cruise missiles and wide-

bodied cruise missile carrier aircraft. Such a "slow" counterforce capability might be an attractive option to those who believe that the United States should have the capability to respond in kind to a Soviet counterforce attack but should, at the same time, avoid posing a potentially destabilizing first-strike threat to Soviet strategic forces. (p. 49)[2]

However, military specialists later observed that the government had miscalculated the Soviet reaction to the threat posed by the cruise:

Soviet leaders give no indication that they view cruise missiles as less dangerous than other, faster weapons; indeed, it is uncertain how far they accept the prevalent American conceptual distinction between first- and second-strike weapons.

This observer pointed out that:

An official Soviet publication argues that a cruise missile cannot be detected when launched or in flight. "Consequently it is also a first-strike weapon like Pershing 2." (p. 19)[3]

Canada's attractiveness as a test site for the cruise, in the eyes of the Pentagon at least, was obvious: Canada is on the short route to the USSR, and the proposed test area has the same geographic characteristics (flat, relatively featureless) as the Soviet target areas. The United States' awareness that the Soviets had developed their own version of the cruise contributed to the urgency for the tests.

The first test of the American cruise missile over Canada took place on March 7, 1984 over northeast Alberta despite profound reservations about the tests offered by Canadian citizens, some of whom carried their concerns to the streets in protest marches. Sympathetic protests were held by antinuclear and other groups in the United States and Europe. The Canadian decision to allow the cruise tests was fraught with political contradictions, among them the fact that Pierre Trudeau and his government approved the test plan during the period in which the prime minister was pursuing his globe-trotting peace initiative. Canadian military officials at the time concluded that Trudeau supported the tests in order to develop credibility and leverage with Washington.[4] It seems ironic, therefore, that the Reagan Administration's reward to Trudeau for his having engineered the approval for the cruise tests was, in its most positive manifestation, a cool public response to his peace initiative. In fact, Reagan's reaction to the peace initiative revealed fully the bristling antagonism that permeated Canadian/American relations for the period. U.S. Undersecretary of State for Political Affairs, Lawrence S. Eagleberger characterized Trudeau's peace initiative as the product of marijuana-induced fantasizing.[5] There were charges from administration officials that Canada, under Trudeau, had not done its part in supporting NATO. The Reagan Administration's charges were made despite Trudeau's approval of the cruise tests in the face of unprecedented domestic and international pressure against the tests. Once again, Canada's military role had emerged as a full-fledged bilateral concern. And it emerged in the midst of an American administration characterized by unflinchingly nationalistic political discourse. A major challenge for Canada in the cruise test decision was how to negotiate a stance that would symbolize Canada's contribution to the defense of the continent and its support for NATO without jeopardizing its sovereignty as perceived by the larger international community.

The present analysis reveals the degree to which American journalism reflected the international, particularly the Soviet, response to Canada's role in the cruise tests and the implications of that coverage for the discourse that was brought to bear on America's policy for testing the cruise in Canada. Simply put, the key question is as follows: Did the American press inform its consumers about the international response to the cruise test proposal and invite them to ponder the policy implications of that response for Canadian/American relations?

The principle of national sovereignty, established in the Peace of Westphalia in 1648, holds that governments are the supreme lawmakers in their own territories. Sovereignty has meaning because there is international recognition of and respect for the right of nations to govern as they wish within their own boundaries, enter into treaties with other nations and formulate their own foreign policies.[6] Sovereignty exists, is honored and changes character by virtue of international communications. Journalistic accounts of international affairs contribute significantly to perceptions of relative sovereignty among nations.

Most commentators treat sovereignty in defensive, nationalistic terms and assess the political health of a nation on the basis of a government's ability to overcome threats posed by external forces. Some, on the other hand, argue that exaggerated concerns for national sovereignty stand in the way of international collaboration in such enterprises as environmental protection. Their arguments underscore the need to understand how journalists' definitions of sovereignty help or hinder communications that contribute to public internationalism. Caldwell, for one, expressed the concern that:

> The concept of sovereignty and exclusive jurisdiction inherent in conventional political thought works against compromise and against giving equal weight to sometimes diffuse ecological considerations as opposed to specific economic interests of a government's political constituents. (p. 209)[7]

One view of Canada's sovereignty is captured in Holmes comment that:

> our record since the last war of balancing a common international interest against domestic pressures has on the whole been good, although the public and politicians often find the juggling hard to tolerate. Our American friends sincerely profess their respect in principle for some nonconformity of allies but find a human difficulty in accepting it when it is actually practiced. (p. 84)[8]

Canada's diplomatic "juggling" involving its relations with the United States is routinely understood as a "counterweight strategy." The delicate nature of this strategy is apparent in Clarkson's evaluation of the irony inherent in the logic of Canada committing to the cruise tests as part of its NATO obligation:

> NATO is generally cited as the classic example of Canada's using an international organization to offset its satellitic relationship, but subscribing to NATO strategy can force it back into further bilateral dependence. Canada's agreement to permit the United States to test its cruise missile on the Primrose Range in northeastern Alberta was a case in point. It could be seen as an example of counter-weight to the extent that the introduction of a new generation of American missiles was a collective NATO decision to respond to the Soviet Union's installation of the SS-20 counterforce missile in eastern Europe. To the extent that it represented an adoption by Canada of the Reagan administration's extreme cold war strategy — Prime Minister Trudeau justified the cruise missile testing on the grounds that "we must also show the Soviet Union that we can meet them gun for gun if necessary" — it showed a vicious circle to be in operation, counterweight diplomacy bringing Canada back to bilateral dependence. (p. 281)[9]

Other Canadian observers believe that with the increased sophistication of American missile power, the United States is less likely to respond to Canadian bargaining that is based in assumptions about the strategic, military significance of the location and size of Canada's territory to America's defense planning. Holmes argued that the reality of this change in Canada's bargaining position is demonstrated by the fact that the pressure for sustaining NORAD comes less from the American than the Canadian military (p. 234).[10] Canada's foreign policy has been described as primarily reactive; responding to the policies and actions of other countries.[11] However, Raymond analyzed Canada's foreign policy behavior vis-à-vis Soviet/American relations and concluded that Canada responds independently and reciprocally to Soviet initiatives that are directed specifically to Canada, and that such direct initiatives influence Canada's behavior toward the Soviet Union more than does Canada's conformity with American policy toward the Soviets.[12] In other words, Canada seems to have a history of responding to Soviet initiatives for cooperation independently and reciprocally rather than conforming to American Soviet policy despite the fact that Canada is perceived as a subordinate state in an asymmetrical relationship with the United States. These findings, in the larger context of the assumptions about Canadian sovereignty previously reviewed, invite questions about the role of the international press. If, for example, Canada has a history of responding independently and favorably to Soviet initiatives, how might Canadians respond to Soviet appeals (through the government's international press) to halt the cruise tests? And to what extent does the American press provide its audience access to the nature of the Soviet appeals so that they might better appreciate the international pressures on Canada and thereby take measures to influence U.S. policy that involves Canada's sovereignty?

A CRUISE CHRONOLOGY: THE EVENTS, ISSUES, AND EMERGING ARGUMENTS

In an attempt to understand the role of the press in the cruise missile issue and the implications of that role for American public debate about Canada's participation in the tests, the major events, and the political issues that emerged in the American and foreign press coverage of those events are reviewed here. To the extent possible, they are organized chronologically.[13]

The words of one American cruise missile expert reveal that, from his perspective at least, the public discourse about the cruise was insignificant as an influence on policy. The role of the public is not an issue for this commentator. From his viewpoint, the fate of the cruise rests firmly in the hands of the Washington bureaucracy, unencumbered by public concerns.

> The political aspects most easily controlled by American leaders are internal. In contrast to weapon programs such as the MX, there is negligible controversy about cruise missiles — and thus no appreciable basis for constraint — in the body politic. Only the intragovernmental politics of legislative-executive relations, organizational interests, and bureaucratic bargaining apply. (p. 34)[14]

This observation raises the obvious question about the extent to which the press contributed to the impression of "negligible controversy" for the cruise missile.

In June 1981, a technical document dealing with joint U.S./Canadian weapons testing was given routine approval by the Canadian parliament. The international political significance of this document went unnoticed, for the most part, by Canadian politicians and the press. Some commentators, in their historical analyses of the cruise tests, believe that the implications of this document were overlooked as a result of the politicians' preoccupation with the western economic summit being held in Ottawa at the time.[15] At any rate, this document represents the beginning of the cruise tests as a public political issue.

In the winter and spring of 1983, interest in cruise testing became a major issue in Canada after half a million people demonstrated in Vancouver and other Canadian cities. In June and July 1983, similar demonstrations were held in American cities including New York and several west coast locations. Several issues were associated with these protests and the press coverage of them. The international press coverage, especially those reports from eastern bloc countries raised the question of complicity very early in the history of the cruise testing proposal. In fact, on January 22, 1983, the Havana International Service issued the first foreign press report to suggest that America co-opted the Canadians into larger U.S. military strategies.

On February 10, 1983, Canada and the United States signed the 5-year weapons tests agreement in Washington, DC. The so-called "Test and Evaluation Plan" was valid for 5 years and could be extended another 5 years upon agreement by both governments. On the occasion of this signing, Alan MacEachen, Minister of External Affairs for the Trudeau government, contended that the tests were part of Canada's commitment to NATO. The *New York Times* report of February 11, 1983 is the first of the world presses to report that Canadian officials saw the tests as part of that country's NATO commitment.

> In Parliament, Mr. MacEachen defended the testing agreement, the unpopularity of which he had earlier acknowledged when he insisted that it was intimately linked to Canada's security as a member of the North Atlantic Treaty Organization. He also said that the test agreement in no way clashed with the government's policy on arms control and disarmament. (*New York Times*, Friday, February 11, 1983)

The Soviet press responded to the logic of cruise tests as a demonstration of Canada's NATO commitment with a series of arguments. On February 15, 1983 Pravda appealed to, invoked Canadian public opinion, linking the tests with the buildup of both NORAD and NATO. The language of that report, a portent of things to come in the Soviet coverage, attached itself firmly to the issue of Canadian sovereignty:

> The Land of the Maple Leaf must not become a testing ground for U.S. nuclear missile preparations which jeopardize not only the cause of preserving peace throughout the world but also Canada's own national security.

One of the charges that emerged from the Soviet press pointed to the hypocrisy represented by Trudeau's allowing the tests in light of his "strategy of suffocation" speech at the United Nations in 1978, in which he argued for a halt to weapons research as a way of curtailing the arms race. A report in the March 3, 1983 *Krasnaya Zvezda* played further on the apparent contradiction. The report begins by quoting the *Toronto Star;* it is another example of the recurring Soviet press strategy of rhetorical legitimization by infusing its arguments with Canadian domestic press discourse:

> The new U.S./Canadian agreement marks a further major change in Ottawa's military-political course. This was emphasized in particular by the *Toronto Star,* Canada's largest newspaper. It reminded readers recently that at the U.N. General Assembly first special session on disarmament the country's Prime Minister P. [*sic*] Trudeau called on all states to pursue a "strategy of stifling nuclear weapons" and to ban the testing of new delivery vehicles. If Canada now takes part in cruise missile tests, the newspaper points out, it will be committing "a regrettable act of hypocrisy."

Later, during the summer, a letter to the editor of the *New York Times* picked up the theme of Trudeau's hypocrisy. The letter is reproduced here in its entirety to demonstrate how reader response has the potential to enjoin world journalistic discourse and foreign policy as one example of public internationalism and how its persuasibility and form compare to the other press examples.

New York Times August 5, 1983
An Abandoned Stance Against the Arms Race

To the Editor:

The Canadian Government's decision to allow U.S. testing of unarmed air-launched cruise missiles (ALCM's) at the Primrose Lake Weapons Range in Alberta directly contradicts Canada's "suffocation" disarmament policy and undermines the prospects of achieving a U.S.-Soviet ban on advanced cruise missile technology.

In 1978 and 1982 at the United Nations, Prime Minister Trudeau outlined a strategy to "suffocate" the arms race, which included a ban on flight-testing of new strategic weapons. Now he suggests that for Canada to refuse the testing of U.S. missiles on its territory would be a violation of NATO unity and have no connection whatsoever to the NATO decision to station ground-launched cruise missiles in Europe.

The testing and deployment of this dangerous, accurate weapon designed for nuclear war-fighting is more likely to spur the Soviet Union to accelerate its own cruise missile program to catch up with the United States rather than help bring about an arms control agreement. It represents a unilateral escalation of the arms race.

Polls show that more than 50 percent of the Canadian people oppose the testing of ALCM's; important elements of the church, labor and arms control communities across Canada urged Trudeau to refuse to allow the testing scheduled to begin this winter. By ignoring this opportunity to take a specific step to "suffocate" the arms race, Canada has chosen instead to become an active partner in the nuclear competition between the superpowers.

Mike Jendrzjczyk
Disarmament Director
Fellowship of Reconciliation
Nyack, N.Y., July 25, 1983[16]

Meanwhile, other world press services responded to the suggestion that the tests were part of Canada's NATO role. On February 20, 1983, the Chinese News service Remnin Ribao, Beijing, pointed out that the move flew in the face of Canadian public opinion.

Heedless of strong domestic opposition to the move, the Canadian government has insisted on allowing the tests of U.S. cruise missiles on Canadian territory, in order to fulfill Canada's obligations to NATO and the North American Air Defense Joint command and ensure the country's security. The Canadian government took another factor into consideration when taking this step. It hoped in this way to stimulate the talks on limiting medium-range nuclear weapons and reduce the danger of nuclear war.

This report, unlike the Soviet treatment, went on to provide a comprehensive view of the logic driving the Canadian political discourse about the test issue by isolating the opposing arguments about cruise tests in the Canadian political establishment. The logic is interpreted as follows: The Conservatives agreed on the basis of collective defense agreements—NATO, NORAD; the Liberal party agreed on the basis of world tensions, especially Soviet intrusions in Afghanistan. The significance of this coverage is that the world press, including pro- and anti-Soviet sources, recognized and apparently accepted Canada's argument that the tests were a necessary part of her commitment to NATO. One of the Reagan Administration's major reasons for its lackluster response to Trudeau's peace initiative was its belief that Canada wasn't pulling its weight in NATO. That argument loses force in light of the international political press' awareness of Canada's NATO commitment argument.

On March 23 and 24, 1983, Vice President Bush visited Canada to discuss trade, acid rain, and cruise testing. Eggs were thrown at him by anti-war-missile protestors. Pierre Trudeau, speaking at a dinner for Bush, said that Canada, as a NATO member, cannot refuse requests of the Europeans, its NATO allies. During these talks, Bush said that the United States had not formally asked Canada to allow cruise tests. Press accounts of Bush's visit varied in their treatment of his claim that the U.S. was not pressuring Canada for the tests. The Soviet newspaper *Tass,* in a March 24, 1983 report, argued several points in response to the Bush visit to Canada. First, the cruise is a first strike weapon; there are plans to deploy it in Western Europe, and that "[t]he aim is not 'reduction of nuclear armaments' as Bush claims but development of that offensive first-strike weapon before its deployment in Western Europe and other parts of the world." On this same day, the Moscow Domestic Service argued that the purpose of Bush's visit was to "get Canada's final agreement on the tests in Alberta and to get unconditional support for Reagan's so-called 'zero option.' "

On April 23, 1983, the *Washington Post* reported that Trudeau said that his decision to permit the actual cruise tests depends on how the U.S. explains its lack of progress on arms limitation talks at Geneva. He admitted that a memorandum of understanding had been signed the week before. This was the first suggestion in the non-Canadian press of Trudeau's using the cruise tests as a bargaining chip.

On April 25, 1983, the *New York Times* reported that some 50,000 anti-cruise protestors demonstrated in Toronto and Vancouver. Meanwhile, the April 29, 1983 report from the Chinese News Service Xinhua, summarizing Trudeau's visit to Washington to prepare for the Williamsburg economic visit, notes that Trudeau told Vice President Bush that the proposed testing of the cruise was becoming a "serious and deeply troubling issue" for the Canadian government. The foreign reports, much more than those in the American press, raise fully the issue of the role of cruise testing in Canada's international political bargaining.

On May 14, 1983, the Montreal Information Service reported that Mikhail Gorbachev, then a member of the CPSU Central Committee, and chairman of the Legislative Proposals Commission of the USSR Supreme Soviet, would lead a Soviet delegation to Canada to discuss agriculture, bilateral relations, the arms race and the Soviet presence in Afghanistan. The May 19, 1983 Pravda report summarizing Gorbachev's speech to the Canadian Parliament quotes him as follows:

We are in favor of closing all channels of the strategic arms race. Guided by this, the Soviet Union has proposed that the USSR and the United States adopt a mutual commitment not to deploy a new kind of strategic weapon — long range cruise missiles. The U.S. refusal of such an agreement testifies to an intention to develop its strategic offensive potential even further. We cannot fail to draw the corresponding conclusions from this.

There was no reference to this Soviet proposal on American network television or in the American prestige print press surveyed for the period of this study. In the context of the pending cruise tests at this particular time (no tests had yet occurred), this proposal had significant policymaking potential as a part of the public political discourse between Canada, the United States, and the Soviets. Its exclusion from the American press effectively removed it from the larger public forum and the consequent influence of that discourse on defense policy for politically responsive audience members who might not have access to this information through alternative press or governmental channels. Political disaggregation among anti-cruise activists was likely forestalled by the failure of the American press to report Gorbachev's nondeployment cruise proposal and to acknowledge the international political significance of the Canadian press in response to Gorbachev's visit.[17] Meanwhile, headlines across Canada summarized the major topics associated with the Gorbachev visit. The domestic news reports provided considerable detail about Canada's intermediary role in U.S.-Soviet relations. A brief sample of some of the many headlines in the Canadian press for the period reveals the tone of the reportage, the geographical scope and general significance of the Gorbachev visit for Canadians:

"Soviet Leader in Ottawa Assails U.S." (*Globe and Mail,* May 17, 1983)

"U.S. Policies Boosting Tensions: Soviet Leader" (*Montreal Gazette,* May 17, 1983)

"Visiting Soviet Blames U.S. for Nations' Hostile Relations" (*Winnipeg Free Press,* May 17, 1983)

"PM's Criticism's Likely to Miff U.S. but Please Soviets" (*Winnipeg Free Press,* May 17, 1983)

"Top Soviet Faults U.S. for Tension." "Washington Silent Over PM's Remarks" The latter story reveals the characteristic "No response" phenomenon typical of both the American Press and the Administration regarding Canada's intermediary role (*Calgary Herald,* both May 17, 1983)

"Visiting Russian Leader Knocks U.S. Propaganda" (*Globe and Mail,* May 18, 1983)

"Messages Sent via Trudeau." This story quotes a senior external affairs officials as saying that Prime Minister Trudeau is acting as an informal mediary between the Soviets and U.S. President Reagan (*Winnipeg Free Press,* May 19, 1983)

"Soviets, U.S. Must Share Blame" (*Halifax Chronicle Herald,* May 18, 1983)

"Trudeau Invited to Visit Soviet Union," and "McKinnon says Gorbachev admits Deploying SS-20s" (*Globe and Mail,* May 19, 1983)

In May 1983, Pierre Trudeau was interviewed by the *Toronto Star.* The interview included several questions about the significance of Canada's defense policy for Soviet/American relations. The interview received international press attention and the use of that material by the many presses represented in the news sample is, in itself, a case study of the way the press selectively constructs international political reality. *Tass,* for example, in its May 16, 1983 report, selected as its focal point Trudeau's remarks about President Reagan being the target of the Canadian citizen protests against the cruise:

Trudeau said:

[t]he majority of the Canadians holding protest demonstrations against cruise missiles are protesting the policy of the American President, whom they consider a militarist or someone so hostile toward the Soviet Union that he cannot be trusted. Unfortunately, President Reagan and some of his entourage have given certain grounds for such misgivings.

On nuclear questions, the prime minister continued:

I disagree with the United States on many things. The United States must conduct a dialogue with the Soviet Union and must recognize that the USSR has its own strategic interests which it wants to defend. The Soviet Union is "a great power" and it must be treated as a great power. I do not consider those people in or close to the U.S. Administration who believe that pressure can be brought to bear on the Soviet Union to be realists.

And, significantly, this Soviet report acknowledges Trudeau's argument that the cruise tests are for the purpose of demonstrating its commitment to NATO:

At the same time, Trudeau came out in support of the Canadian Government's intention to allow the United States to use Canadian territory to test cruise missiles. "The reasons Canada reached a broad accord with the United States, which might or might not lead to tests of cruise missiles," he declared, "are connected to a considerable degree with NATO policy. . . . This is something we are doing with regard to NATO's dual decision."

Meanwhile, the *Los Angeles Times* report of May 22, 1983 includes Trudeau's explanation for the demonstrations, along with a detailed map of the proposed test site. It too quotes Trudeau as saying the tests will allow

Canada to do its part in NATO but defines that role as defensive in nature: "to counter the Soviet buildup of the SS-20's." There is no mention of Trudeau's call for a Soviet/American dialogue or his plea for America to recognize the basis of the Soviet's need to protect their interests.

On July 16, 1983, the *New York Times* announced that the Canadian government had formally approved the tests. External Affairs Minister McEachen is reported as again having said that the tests are for the purposes of western security. The Canadian House vote on this issue is revealed; 213 for, 34 against with the NDP opposed. The *Los Angeles Times* report on that same day, in passing, mentions the issue of the threat posed to environmental safety, an issue that gains importance, especially in the Soviet Press, as the tests proceed.[18] The Soviet press response based its appeals in the (Canadian and American governments') disregard for Canadian public opinion. The July 24, 1983 report from *Tass* is representative: "By yielding to Washington's demands, the Canadian Government has thus openly disregarded the country's public opinion which resolutely opposed such a step." And its quotation from the newspaper *Izvestia* contains a weapons-freeze proposal and the sharpest attack (usually reserved for the Americans) on the Canadian government in the Soviet news examples:

> The real way to peace, the newspaper IZVESTIYA points out, lies through a nuclear weapons freeze, through disarmament based on equality and equal security. "By its consent to American missile tests in Alberta Province, Ottawa has shown that it does not see or does not wish to see that way."

Shortly after the tests were approved, the Soviet press focused its rhetoric on the safety threat posed by the tests. It constructed its arguments by reviewing a litany of incidents that demonstrate the United States' tendency toward environmental ignorance, including acid rain, agent orange and missile accidents in Europe. The United States used agent orange from 1974–78 to remove dense vegetation along the Canadian/American border. NBC–TV news ran the story on August 7, 1983. The story was unusually long for television; three minutes and forty seconds. *Tass* summarized the story on August 8, 1983 to warrant the claim that: "This latest report shows that the interests and health of both U.S. citizens and of neighboring countries are deeply alien to U.S. ruling circles." The use of this story by the Soviet and American press in different rhetorical contexts reveals several characteristics of international news form; that news services frequently monitor each other for news material, and that, ultimately, all news thrives on dramatic material, regardless of the persuasive work it is expected to accomplish. The symbolic power of the image of the contaminated border was mutually attractive to the American and Soviet reporters.

One of the most detailed pieces of American reportage associated with the cruise issue was written by David Hoffman in the *Washington Post* on March 12, 1985. This is one of the rare instances in which the American press cites a Canadian publication. The story introduces what was to become one of the most significant political issues associated specifically with the cruise missile, and more generally, American missile policy with regard to Canada: the issue of deployment and Canadian sovereignty. The report begins by referring to an interview in the Canadian magazine *Maclean's:*

President Reagan told the Canadian magazine *Maclean's* that the United States would not deploy nuclear weapons in Canada without the permission of its government. Reagan responded to reports that contingency plans exist to deploy nuclear weapons in Canada and elsewhere.

Reagan said that "over the years NATO has worked out various defense plans designed to strengthen deterrence. But, under these plans, any deployments would be carried out only, with the prior agreement of the states involved. The president added that it is contrary to the interest of the alliance and to the individual member states to talk "publically" about such contingency plans. The reports of their existence has stirred controversy in Canada; Reagan is to visit Quebec City next weekend for a meeting with Prime Minister Brian Mulroney. Reagan also said that although he would welcome Canada's participation in his Strategic Defense Initiative, "We have absolutely no intention of pressing any of our allies to participate in this program."

This addresses the very charge in the earlier Soviet piece suggesting that U.S. missiles were to be deployed in countries without their permission. The comparison discloses the importance of these news reports as interactive discursive elements in making informed political judgments about the cruise issue. The question addressed by this report and raised repeatedly in the Soviet press is: "Will the cruise and other nuclear missiles be deployed in Canada?" The deployment policy for the cruise was not clear. In fact, the strategic use of the cruise in bargaining and the nature of the deployment of the weapon had been topics of heated discussion in Washington:

On the basis of the logic of the "action–reaction" syndrome, some within the U.S. government bureaucracy are prepared to support U.S. cruise missile programs, but only for use as a "bargaining chip" in SALT II, not for actual deployment. Even as the inherent military value of the cruise missile manifested itself early in the advanced developmental stage, controversy over the future of the weapons system erupted among the Pentagon, Department of State and the White House as well as within the Pentagon itself. (p. 45)[19]

The credibility of the Reagan Administration was strained on this point when the American Defense Secretary Casper Weinberger addressed the issue during a visit to Canada. His remarks were hardly reassuring for the Canadians. But the U.S. credibility problem was exacerbated when his comments were eliminated from a Pentagon transcript of his speech and the editing was explained as a "typist's error." The *Washington Post* reported the flap on March 20, 1985:

> A day after Defense Secretary Weinberger aroused Canadian sensitivities by raising the possibility of deploying U.S. missile defenses in Canada, the Pentagon released a transcript yesterday that omitted his controversial remarks.
>
> A U.S. Embassy spokesman in Ottawa, where the transcript was prepared, explained that 11 key words were "inadvertently dropped by an office typist."

This same report, in conjunction with the news coverage of Reagan's promise not to deploy, raises the question of whether the omissions were made because of the potential of Weinberger's words to create diplomatic problems:

> Weinberger, speaking in an interview Monday with Canadian television after the two nations signed a new agreement on joint air defense, was asked if U.S.–Canadian defense against Soviet cruise missiles might mean placing American weapons on Canadian soil.
>
> "I don't have any idea as to where the defense would be placed" Weinberger replied. "They would be first placed in the most effective way. But I think what we would try to do would be to locate the best places for defense. Some might be here, some might be in the United States, some might be at sea."
>
> Twenty-four hours later, a Pentagon [*sic*] official handed out a transcript of the interview omitting reference to possible locations for the defenses.
>
> "It was absolutely a fluke error" explained Stan Zuckerman, the U.S. Embassy spokesman, adding that it is "Weird" that the omissions covered only the controversial portion of the interview. He said a secretary had mistakenly dropped the line while typing the transcript, which was later cabled to Washington.
>
> Weinberger's remarks, coming at the end of President Reagan's visit to Quebec, raised a small flurry because some Canadian politicians have charged that the new air defense agreement might commit Canada to accepting U.S. weapons.

Targeting Canada As "Ground Zero"

Soviet appeals repeatedly stress the horrific irony of the United States using Canada for testing as an analogue to Soviet geography. The implication in these particular news constructions, which pervade the Soviet news as a theme, is that by using Canada as a substitute target the United States is being abusive, hostile to both Canada and the Soviet Union; that these tests violate a shared northern culture. To this end, the Soviets construct complex, often lyrical appeals and honorific labels for Canada as in this Soviet commentary from Moscow's Krasnaya Zvezda on July 1, 1985:

"The Canadian sky is blue and the rain falls on birch trees, just like in Russia . . ." the Soviet popular song about Canada runs. Yet increasingly often the land of the Maple Leaf where the birch trees are like Russian birch trees, is showered with destructive acid rain, produced by atmospheric pollution from industrial enterprises in the United States, hears the thunder of exploding bombs and shells used by NATO forces as they rehearse methods of waging aggressive wars on Canadian firing ranges, and see the ominous shadows of U.S. cruise missiles and B-25 [sic] strategic bombers as they fly past.

Examples of other Soviet labels and metaphors that are repeatedly used by *Tass* portraying Canada as a target for U.S. objectives include:

"Cruise death" (Moscow *Pravda,* 3/7/84)

"U.S. will tighten still further the 'noose of military cooperation' around the neck of its closest neighbor and partner in NATO and NORAD (Moscow *Pravda,* 3/13/84)

Canada as "Mandate Territory" same report, (Moscow *Pravda,* 3/13/84)

Canada as "Pentagon appendage," "Reagan and his hegemonistic plans," (Moscow *Tass,* 11/2/84)

"A Test Range of the Pentagon," "the peace-endangering preparations of the U.S. government," both in (Moscow *Tass,* 2/26/85)

Canadians As Cruise Directors

In Canadian, Soviet, and American coverage, Canadians are the press spokespersons, public relations personnel, the apparent agents in control of the tests: "Canadian spokesman say the development of the technology just wasn't keeping pace with Air Force planning schedules" (*Montreal Domestic Service,* 3/7/84).

Ironically, the American press cites a Canadian spokesperson to answer one of the recurrent concerns raised in the Soviet press; the matter of safety: "A Canadian official said the test could easily be aborted if the missile wandered off-course" (*New York Times,* 1/21/86).

Canadian armed forces are reported as being intricately involved in the tests in the American and Soviet press. The *New York Times* reported that

"Two Canadian Forces f-18 jets will attempt to locate and intercept the missile in its five and a half hour flight" (*New York Times,* 1/21/86).

After one of the crashes of free-flight cruises the *Washington Post* reported:

> In Ottawa, Associate Defense Minister Harvie Andre said the crash occurred when the missile's engine failed to ignite after the launch, Reuters reported. [Note use of international press, rare for the U.S. Press.] (*Washington Post,* 2/26/86)

And the *New York Times* account revealed that:

> "Debris was spread over an area about 100 feet in diameter where the missile crashed Tuesday after being dropped from a B-52 bomber," a Canadian Forces spokesman, Captain Ross Hick's said. Then later . . . "The recovery operation could take several days with work delayed by daytime temperatures of 4 degrees below zero," said Fred Harrop of the United States Air Force. He said the recovery team had American military personnel helped by Canadian military and policemen. (*New York Times,* 2/27/86)

Harvie Andre and Hicks, the Canadian spokespersons are the key players in explaining the crash to the press. On October 7, 1986, the Canadian Defense Minister announced that tests would resume. The tests had been interrupted since February 26, 1986; a period of 8 months. A *Washington Post* report makes it clear that the Canadians were in control of the decision to suspend the tests:

> U.S. military officials announced they will resume testing unarmed cruise missiles Tuesday over the frozen terrain of northwestern Canada. Environmentalists said they would try to scuttle the plan. Canada suspended testing of the missiles a year ago after two of them crashed in Canada. Yesterday Ottawa agreed to allow resumption of the tests. (*Washington Post,* 2/23/87)

The recurring Soviet charges of Canada having been compromised by the Americans seem to be warranted by the revelations that the Canadians are closely involved in and serving as spokespersons for the tests. On the other hand, the Soviets' suggestion that the Canadians are unwittingly being exploited by the Americans loses force in light of this recurring pattern in the reports.

Political Linkage As Argument

Soviet commentators linked the cruise tests with a number of other issues in Canadian/American relations. Among them were:

U.S. Trade; "the Canadians will be pressured about the cruise at the Williamsburg (economic summit)," (Moscow *Tass*, 4/29/83)

The ongoing Soviet/American disarmament talks; one example, suggesting that Canadians, by virtue of public opinion and protests, are against both the cruise and the deployment of Pershing II's in Europe. (Moscow *Pravda*, 5/21/83)

Canadian nuclear free zone movements. (See for example (Moscow *Domestic Service*, 6/17/83, 11/29/83 and 2/25/85)

Canadian aircraft losses due to Americans selling substandard aircraft. (Moscow *Tass*, July 12, 1983)

Environmental issues were linked to the tests in both the American and Soviet press although pursued more aggressively by the Soviets. This linkage involved the following specific issues:

Acid Rain—(The *Washington Post* makes such a connection in its review of Reagan's *Maclean Magazine* interview-3/12/85) (*Zvezda*, 7/1/85 also makes the acid rain-cruise connection)

Agent orange-Moscow's *Tass* (see August 8, 1983) used the argument of U.S. environmental abuse.

The safety of the tests, i.e. as accident, regardless of environmental impact (Moscow *Tass*, 3/2/84)

The *Montreal Domestic Service* raised the question, "Why are the tests much less extensive than the original schedule called for? Are their problems in the testing program?" (3/7/84). This prompted a reply from Captain Marty Tate of the Cold Lake Base to say that the schedule is being put together with safety as a top priority.

The safety issue was linked with the deployment of the Pershing Missile in the Federal Republic of Germany by the Soviet press (Moscow *Domestic Service*, 1/18/85). Another report warns of "a tragic mistake; the Pentagon can't guarantee against such a thing happening" (Moscow *Pravda*, 2/21/85). In this connection the American press reported after a free flight crash of a cruise, "It crashed at least ten miles off target, officials said, adding that it posed no danger" (*New York Times*, 1/23/86). Later, American press commentary acknowledged that after these mishaps, the Canadians were reluctant to grant continued permission for the next series of tests and did so only after explanations for the mishaps were given (Herbert Denton in the *Washington Post*, 11/10/86). For the most part, the cruise test difficulties were treated as domestic industrial product issues by the American press. An excerpt from a July 3rd report from the *Washington Post* demonstrates the tendency:

The Air Force, recently stung by public revelations of shortcomings in the B1 bomber and MX missile programs, has begun an investigation into suspected defects in its nuclear-tipped air launched cruise missiles, or ALCMs, Air Force officials and congressional sources said yesterday. The investigation centers on allegations that a key part of the cruise missile has been improperly tested by its manufacturer, the Northrop Corp., calling into question the missile's ability to hit their targets in the Soviet Union in the event of a nuclear war, the officials said. Northrop announced yesterday that it had removed four employees at the Pomona, Calif.' plant that produced the parts, "pending the outcome of an investigation begun last week into possible irregularities in the testing of electronic components." Law enforcement sources in Washington confirmed that the Justice Department's Fraud Section and the FBI are investigating the allegations. Northrop has produced the component in question-known as an "altitude stabilization unit" and intended to keep the missile on course during high-speed, low-level flights over Soviet territory-for half of the roughly 1,800 cruise missiles in the U.S. strategic arsenal, according to congressional and industry sources. Most of the missiles are deployed on B-52 strategic bombers. (*Washington Post, 7/3/86*)[20]

The Soviet press argued repeatedly that the cruise and the NATO tests in which Canada participated must be seen as a sign of a general build-up toward a nuclear confrontation as engineered by the United States: "Yet another evidence of Washington's endeavors to draw the land of the "Maple Leaf" deeper into U.S. military preparations (Moscow *Tass*, 2/19/85).

A January 3, 1985 report from *Pravda* points out that the West German Bundeswehr are also using Canadian soil to test tanks:

Air force formations from Britain and other North Atlantic bloc countries are rehearsing low altitude flights in the Goose Bay area. More and more Canadians are becoming aware of how dangerous the war preparations are; they are not reassured by official statements that such exercises are part of Canada's commitment to NATO.

Curiously absent from the U.S. coverage until quite late in the discussion of cruise tests is speculation about the status and development of the Soviet cruise. It does show up in a story about the proposed Canadian sub fleet, that acknowledges that the Canadians want the subs to prevent further violations of their Northwest Passage by the Americans and Soviets:

Canada, hoping to keep the United States and the Soviet Union out of its arctic waters, may build nuclear-powered attack submarines to shore-up its northern defense.

Defense and External Affairs officials agree that a larger, longer term threat comes from the Soviet Union which could begin to deploy submarine-launched cruise missiles this year. (Washington Post, May 3, 1987)

Public Opinion as a Rhetorical Element: In Search
of the Canadian Domestic Perspective

The Soviets routinely appeal to and invoke Canadian public opinion. Their commentaries rarely accuse the people of Canada of policy improprieties. At most, they suggest that the Canadian people are being misled by their government, with the qualification that their government is behaving improperly because of pressure from the U.S. government, as this commentary from Moscow *Krasnaya Zvezda* March 3, 1983 illustrates:

> While stepping up the development and adoption of such weapons, the United States has long been trying to obtain from Canada the right to test cruise missiles at the Primrose Lake test range near the border between the Provinces of Alberta and Saskatchewan.
>
> In the anxious Canadian public's opinion, the transformation of the country's territory into a test range for the latest types of U.S. weapons will lead ultimately to the creation of a bridgehead for their deployment and use. . . . That is what is causing alarm to the Canadian public, and alarm which is shared by all who value the cause of peace and the people's security.

The U.S. press also invokes, refers to, and accommodates public opinion and public opinion polls, but not nearly as frequently as the Soviets. Herbert Denton's commentary in the *Washington Post* article of November 10, 1986 is noteworthy because it breaks the usual American press pattern of ignoring the Canadian perspective altogether; it recalls the vast difference between Canadians and Americans in poll results regarding defense spending, evaluations of Reagan policy, and the need for independent Canadian foreign policy. Of the adult Canadians polled, 60% were against cruise testing. The fact that this reference occurs in a piece of commentary, rather than in hard news, is significant for it recalls the pattern of TV news in which the innvocation of Canadian public opinion occurred only in the most subjective examples of TV news coverage, that is, news constructions that strained against "hard news" conventions.

Details of Canadian domestic politics as they relate to the cruise issue are frequently included in both Soviet and other foreign press reports. For example the Chinese News Service Renmin Ribao reported from Beijing on February 20, 1983:

> In 1979, when the Progressive Conservative Party was in power in Canada, based on the requirements of collective defense it agreed to the NATO deployment of land-based cruise missiles in Western Europe. Since the Liberal Party took office again in 1980, in light of the international tensions caused by the Afghan and other incidents, it has consistently attached importance to

strengthening national defense and the part played by Canada in NATO. (Renmin Ribao, 2/20/83)

Similarly, on December 11, 1984 *Tass* reported on the Parliamentary debate on the Canadian government's attitude to the question of a freeze on nuclear arsenals in the world.

Broadbent (NDP) condemning the conservative's obstructionist stand at the U.N., said "They ignore the opinion of the Canadian people." The government was criticized for its course of alliance with Washington and for U.S. cruise missile tests on Canadian territory. (Moscow *Tass,* 12/11/84)

With the exception of the previously cited Denton commentary in the *Washington Post,* the American press provides no insight into the intensity or character of Canadian domestic political debate on this issue or, for that matter, any of the issues reviewed in this study. There is no substantive information about the nature of Canadian political processes and institutions. And there is virtually no ongoing representation of Canada's activity and status in the international community.

REFUSING THE CRUISE: NATIONAL VERSUS INTERNATIONAL ACCOUNTS OF POLITICAL PROTEST

The American press did not cite Soviet or other international press responses to the wide-ranging cruise protests. Excluding the international reaction to the protests has the potential to constrain the critical review of American policy assessment on the part of lobbyists and others concerned about the issue. In addition, by reinforcing the vague and insensitive measures of public opinion that are typically used to legitimate policy, this press myopia might inhibit discussions of alternatives to the policy.

The cruise protests remain a relatively abstract entity in the bulk of the news coverage. Neither the character of the participants nor their political objectives are revealed clearly. As a political force, the protestors are more frequently represented in the Soviet press than the American, where they are used as part of "citizen opinion" appeals that are a routine part of the Soviet response to the tests. The protest activity itself follows a dynamic ebb-and-flow pattern, synchronous with the occurrence of major test events. The Soviet press reports are shaped by the rhythm of the protest activity. For example, on December 2, 1983, *Tass* reported that 26 anti-war groups in Canada asked the Supreme Court to ban the missile tests on the basis that they imperil the lives of Canadians. This event supported the Soviet press logic that the tests were inherently unsafe. And as part of that rhetorical effort, the Soviets recruited the Canadian press. The March 2, 1984 *Tass* report noted that "Canada's Southam news agency says the military is concealing the extent of risk in case of a military accident."

Unlike the Soviets, American journalists showed little interest in pursuing the relationship between the protests and Canadian domestic politics. Most of the coverage in both American television and print was tersely descriptive with overtones of disapproval amidst nationalistic appeals. There were several significant exceptions. The January 22, 1983, *New York Times* had the most extensive American coverage of the protests. The appeals in this news story include invitations for involvement by interested activists, and references to Canadian domestic politics mixed with discussions of overall military policy. And the report, unlike many of the other domestic news stories of the cruise protests, is not wrapped up in American nationalistic symbols. Again, commentary by an individual journalist invites a political response moreso than conventional "hard news" treatment. Excerpts from the report suggest that protest activity has an impact on the policymakers' public relations strategies, if not on policymaking per se:

New York Times, January 22, 1983

Canada-U.S. Pact on Missile Tests is Delayed

By Michael T. Kaufman

Ottawa—Political pressure from an increasingly assertive disarmament movement has delayed the signing of an agreement with the United States to permit testing of unarmed cruise missiles in northern Alberta.

Tacitly acknowledging the unpopularity of the test, Defense Minister Giles Lamontagne said Cabinet ministers would now have to travel and explain the decision "because there seems to be a lot of misinformation."

Such statements are not likely to mollify disarmament activists like church leaders who asked Mr. Trudeau to declare Canada a nuclear-free zone, refuse to test delivery weapons and ban the production of components for nuclear weapons systems. (*New York Times,* 1/22/83)

On December 16, 1983, Prime Minister Trudeau took his peace mission to Washington. The Soviet response to Trudeau's lack of success is an important media intersection; the appeals used here are very similar to those used in the U.S. TV network coverage of the National Film Board issue; the appeals are built on the pretense of defending Canada's best interests when the primary rhetorical force of the construction is to enhance the news organization's credibility by attacking policy. This news report on December 23, 1983 from *Tass* represents the pattern of Soviet response for this issue:

> Ottawa is indignant at U.S. Undersecretary of State Eagleberger's remark that Trudeau's peace efforts were those of a "marijuana-prompted erratic leftist." The remark shows Washington lacks "moral inhibition" even towards its closest allies especially if they disagree with U.S. interventionist policy. Insults do not add to U.S. prestige but serve to show the country's leaders as "apologists of brute force, threats and blackmail in international relations." (Moscow *Tass*, 12/23/83)

The first test of the cruise over Canadian airspace occurred on March 4, 1984. The B-52 left Grand Forks North Dakota before dawn, flew to the Arctic, and circled there until a federal court in Ottawa rejected anti-nuclear activists' arguments that the tests were a danger to people in the test corridor. Four missiles were aboard and remained attached to the B-52 during the 1,500-mile flight that was for the purpose of testing the cruise guidance system. Both the *New York Times* and the *Los Angeles Times* reported this test mentioning the details of the court case that temporarily halted the operation. The March 4, 1984 *Los Angeles Times* report included a picture of protestors from activist organizations, at the Primrose Lake range, one of whom wore a jacket with the slogan "Canada is *not* the 51st State!" prominently displayed on his back. The *New York Times* story mentioned that a narrower legal anti-cruise argument based on Canada's then 2-year-old Charter of Rights was being pursued in the courts by Project Dismantle.

Meanwhile, the protesters plied their legal case until, ultimately on May 13, 1985, the Montreal International Service reported to the world that the Canadian Supreme Court had ruled against the protesters:

> The Supreme Court of Canada ruled today that the courts have the right to review government decisions if they infringe upon rights guaranteed by the Canadian Charter or Rights and Freedom. The decision grew out of a case brought before the court by a coalition of peace and disarmament groups. They claim that a Cabinet decision to allow the United States to test cruise missiles over Northern Canada violates the part of the Charter of Rights and Freedoms which guarantees Canadians the right to life, liberty and security of person. According to the groups the tests increase the risk of nuclear war and so threaten the right to life. But the Court dismissed the case, saying there is no link between the Cabinet decision on cruise testing and the growing risk of nuclear war. However, ruling on a broader principle, the Supreme Court said the executive branch of the government, the Cabinet, has a duty to act in accordance with the Rights of the Character. (Montreal International Service, 5/13/85)

Although the ruling went against the immediate interests of the protesters, it suggests future legal strategies in the context of the Charter of Rights and freedoms; as such it is important coordinating information for the international community of peace activists of that period. Significantly, the details of the ruling were not reported in the American press.

The first air-launched, free-flight of the cruise took place on January 19, 1985. Representatives of Greenpeace, an environmental activist organization, tried unsuccessfully to snare the missile in a net suspended from huge gas balloons. Several days later, a second free-flight test ended in a crash 10 miles off target. And on February 26, another cruise crashed into the Beaufort Sea. Each time, officials reassured the press that the missile posed no danger. The Soviets lost no opportunity to use the crashes to confirm their, by now, long-standing argument about the safety of the cruise. Their response was a tour de force of the characteristic features of Soviet news rhetoric including appeals to and invocation of the Canadian public, warrants to support their claims in the form of detailed references to the comments of Canadian domestic political figures, citation of western wire services such as UPI as a source of their information to lend credibility to their reports, historical review as proof of their earlier allegations that the tests were unsafe, and hyperbole through metaphors, for example, "disaster," Canadian territory as "proving ground" and an "enraged Canadian population demanding total termination of the tests." The *Tass* report of February 26, 1986 is typical of a number of responses to the crashes for the period, its significance to this discussion is that it reveals the contexts that were typical of Soviet coverage of cruise protests:

> The Canadian government has decided to suspend the tests of American cruise missiles over the country's territory, a UPI news agency reported today. The Canadian authorities undertook the step after a cruise missile, during a test flight on Tuesday, went out of control immediately after separating from a B-52 plane. A group of Canadian and American military experts left for the fall site in the Sea of Beaufort. Harvie Andre, Canada's minister for national defense, said that the flights will not be resumed until the causes of the disaster are known. Missile tests in January also ended in failure. The Canadian population are enraged over the fact that their territory has been turned into a proving ground for advanced American weapons, and demand total termination of the tests. Jim Fulton of the New Democratic Party demanded that the United States take back its cruise missiles. (Moscow *Tass*, 2/26/86)

The Soviet international press services, both broadcast and print, selectively include the voices of Canadians and Americans who oppose American political policy in general and who, specifically, oppose the cruise tests. Among those represented were: Prime Minister Trudeau (Moscow

Tass, 2/10/84); John Morgan, President of the Canadian Congress for the Defense of Peace and winner of the international Lenin prize (Moscow *Tass,* 1/3/85); Walter Scott of Grand Forks, a spokesperson for the Red River Valley Peaceworkers (Moscow *Tass,* 1/16/85); and Jim Fulton of the New Democratic Party who demanded that the U.S. "take back its cruise missiles" after a crash (Moscow *Tass,* 2/27/86). These anti-cruise sentiments, especially those excerpted from Parliamentary debate, were often taken entirely out of the political context in which they originally occurred. The rhetorical effect of placing these remarks within Soviet press commentary is to attribute support for Soviet policy and ideology that in most cases was not at all intended by those speakers. The prudent politician, so quoted, no doubt has effective strategies for countering those who would intimidate parliamentary debate by unfairly attempting to make political hay out of the fact that an opponent's words had been incorporated into international press commentary in ways that support Soviet ideology.

As mentioned earlier, Herbert Denton's November 10th *Washington Post* commentary is the most detailed and politically provocative (for the American Canada-watcher) piece of American journalism about the cruise tests. It is represented here in its entirety to reveal the context in which the continuing protests were treated:

> A solid majority of Canadians oppose cruise missile testing in this country and opinion here is almost evenly divided over whether the United States or the Soviet Union is the more likely to start a nuclear war, according to a new nationwide poll.
>
> Canadians also strongly indicated a desire for a more independent Canadian foreign policy, with 59 percent saying Prime minister Brian Mulroney follows the lead of President Reagan too often.
>
> The views expressed in the poll conducted November 1–4 by the Angus Reid Association firm of Winnepeg, appear likely to stiffen resistance by Mulroney's government to pure pressure on Canada to increase defense spending and beef up Canada's NATO contingent in Europe.
>
> Although Mulroney is constructing new frigates and buying 138 F18 fighter aircraft, Canada's expenditure on defense, about 2% of gross national product, is lower than that of any NATO ally except Ireland and Luxembourg. Canadians know they can count on the protection of the U.S. nuclear umbrella, do not favor higher taxes to pay for more defense, and support a powerful peace movement.

Note the premise here, that Canadians want to depend on the U.S. umbrella, therefore can afford a strong peace movement.

Peace groups last year forced Mulroney to back away from an early enthusiasm for the U.S. invitation to participate in SDI. Canadian sentiment's contrast markedly with those of Americans. In the aftermath of the Iceland summit, a Washington Post-ABC News survey indicated that more than 60% of Americans approved of Reagan's handling of relations with the Soviet Union and agreed with his decision at Iceland not to accept restrictions on SDI, his space-based antimissile plan, as the condition for eliminating the nuclear ballistic missiles of the two superpowers.

Canadian attitudes seem certain to intensify pressure on Mulroney to halt cruise missile testing over Canada, which has no nuclear arsenal of its own.

With a note of reluctance, the Canadian government granted permission to continue testing unarmed cruise missiles here later this year after receiving explanations for mishaps that occurred last winter. Two missiles veered off course during tests, causing widespread alarm here although populated areas were not threatened.

Sixty percent of the 1,684 adults surveyed in the Reid poll oppose cruise missile testing, including 72% of the women.

Thirty percent said the Soviet Union would most likely be the one to deliberately start a nuclear war, while 25 percent responded that the United States would be the one to launch a first strike. (*Washington Post,* 11/10/86)

This story acknowledges that protestors influence policy decisions. The example also shows that the commentary of informed reporters is both more detailed and politically provocative than forms that follow the conventions of journalistic "objectivity." In this study, the *Washington Post* more than any other press cited, invested its coverage of the cruise issue with commentary. Subjective reporting, as represented in commentary, whether Soviet or American, is inherently more invitational, that is, has the potential to inform political discourse among its users in ways intended to be consistent with political participation in western democracies. In the context of this analysis, "balance and objectivity," often touted by journalism schools and professional journalists as hallmarks of their craft, appear to be more useful as marketing strategies for attracting audiences by enhancing the popular belief in journalists credibility than as functional rhetorical devices for guiding the reporting of international affairs to politically active audiences.

During this period, the American TV news networks covered protests in various ways; there were very few details of the substance or history of the cruise test proposal and virtually no coverage of international opinion about this issue.

TV's Version: Guilt by Association

In the American television network coverage of the cruise there is a recurring form of mythic communication that encourages nationalistic interpretations through the language of pictures, words, and the contextual organization of news items in a way that distinguishes it from the previous examples. Here the language tends to portray politically active Canadians as threatening the American status quo. It identifies them as engaging in criminal activities or riots when, in fact, they are participating in political demonstrations that are legal and consistent with the prevailing norms for political participation in that society. The linear flow of news items, the way in which stories are ordered, makes political meaning. Guilt by association in news constructions has obvious foreign policy implications. In this news there is one particularly striking example of this tendency to define political opposition to perceived national interests as unacceptable, illegal behavior via the "riot myth" (p. 109)[21] "delegitimization" and "status degradation."

> Under certain circumstances, legitimate political minorities are subjected to severe "status degradation" ceremonies, and are lumped with the more marginal groups. They are then subject to quite different forms of public opprobrium, stigmatization, and exclusion. They have been symbolically *de*-legitimated. (p. 267)[22]

The larger news context in which the cruise story is placed contributes significantly to its meaning. An American domestic news story dealing with the criminal behavior of a concert mob in New York City was associated with and used to define the category of peaceful protests and street marches of Canadian citizens against U.S. plans to test the cruise missile over Canadian territory. In this case the news anchor's voice, down to the level of his verbal inflection, suggests that these two instances are in the same category. The text of the U.S. mob story and the cruise protest story are recalled in detail here to show the political force of this news construction. The two stories were presented as a flowing unit with no commercial breaks between them.

> Reporter: Diana Ross's last song for the more than 300,000 in Central Park was "All For One and One For All." But for up to a thousand kids in the crowd the end of her music marked the beginning of their free-for-all.
>
> Pictures: Roaming youth, aftermath of their attacks.
>
> They began to attack people trying to leave as easy moving targets. These people were running from change-snatchers. The rampaging teenagers overran a nearby restaurant attacking an elderly diner who would end up with

seventy-two stitches in his head, stabbing a passerby, and assaulting at least one employee.

Victim: They had, like, 200 people came and rampaged a truck, turned over things, rampaged the restaurant and also destroyed a cash register.

Reporter: On the edge of Central Park the police shot one man whom they say was robbing someone else. The violence sent many running for cover.

Witness (Broken English): People just afraid, go inside and stay there; many people stay in our restaurant — they're waiting when it's finished.

Reporter: In all, eighty-four teenagers would be arrested, but it would take police two hours to get control. Three hundred police had to leave the concert site in commandeered city buses to go after what some today would call "the wolfpacks."

Policeman: They're just a bunch of kids raising hell and ripping off people. It's a possibility anytime you get a large group of people together.

Reporter: From the Central Park concert the unruly gangs drive thirty blocks south to here — Times Square — forcing shopkeepers to lock themselves in their stories for safety, stealing from people they happened to see on the sidewalk.

Witness: There were over 500 running out on the street, muggin' . . .

Witness: Hulligans! Animals!

Reporter: The New York City Police today said they were like an overrun infantry; they insist nothing more could have been done, except to sweep up the mess from this concert and try again on the next one. Jane Wallace, CBS News, New York. (CBS 7/23/83, 2:20)

Anchor: Thousands of Canadians (anchor's vocal emphasis on *Canadians,* implying that they are another example of the type introduced in the previous story) today protested the planned testing of air launched U.S. Cruise missiles in western and northern Canada.

Pictures: orderly, slow-moving, marching crowds with banners.

Anchor: Protesters gathered outside U.S. consulates and urged Prime Minister Trudeau to refuse the cruise. The Canadian government has agreed to allow as many as six test flights a year starting next January. The U.S. officials say that the test area terrain resembles large parts of the Soviet Union. (CBS 7/23/83, :30)

The story immediately following the cruise missile summary reveals further the news logic of story categorization; it begins this way:

Anchor: A lull in the three-year Iran/Iraq war ended today . . . (CBS 7/23/83, :10)

The associational montage of news has the potential to define the anti-cruise demonstration as illegal, threatening, potentially riotous. The news definition of the situation opposes the ideal of legal political protest in democracies. The news stories, in their positioning, set up oppositions including Canada versus the U.S. Canadian civilians are represented as functioning outside the law. The threat of the Canadian protest is set up in the first story with its visual and aural litany of victims; of mobs out of control. Its quick-cutting through a series of victim and witness responses to attacks establishes, through rhythms of disorder, the idea that crowds demonstrating in the street can become mobs out of control. The definition is part of a flow of symbols that, together, gain a compelling linguistic force that favors a particular interpretation. The policeman's words in the concert story: "It's a possibility anytime you get a large group of people together," lend suspicion to the motives of the Canadian demonstrators.

These stories do not reveal much about the different sociopolitical contexts they represent. There are no Canadian spokespersons used to explain the nature or tone of their political concerns. Instead, they are represented visually, and the force of the preceding images makes the association a threatening one.

One is left with the visual association as the primary political definition. A number of significant points that would help the interested viewer define the legitimacy of the Canadian protests are left dangling: What are the political issues? Who has determined that the tests be made? What are the implications of the test for Canada's sovereignty and its international image? What is Trudeau's stand and why?

The grammar of news production and the conventions that lie behind it lump categories of stories together as a matter of routine. In this case, street demonstrations, street violence, and war were associated as a news type. Although the definition of Canadian protest as criminal, extralegal activity can be explained as the result of routine news practices, the meaning for the foreign policymaker is significant. If we assume that the foreign policy elite have a more detailed knowledge of the cruise missile tests than the less politically oriented viewer, the news construction reviewed here could be read in several ways. For example, if one were a supporter of the administration's defense strategies and policies, the conclusion might be that this news report defines opposition to the tests negatively in the public eye and thereby works to the advantage of the cruise test advocates. The policymaker must therefore take action by actively encouraging further supportive strategies for cruise tests. On the other hand, if an audience member were in the opposition ranks with regard to this proposal, this coverage might be read as an indication of the lack of understanding of the threat the tests represent to Canadian/ American relations and the expedientresponse is to move quickly to formulate policy that corrects the public definition of the situation.

Another short report refers to court action but provides no detail of the substance or history of the protest movement.

Anchor: The U.S. Cruise missile had its first test run in Canadian airspace today but it took court action to get the go-ahead. A U.S. Air Force B-52 took off early this morning from Grand Forks, North Dakota for Canada, but it remained in a holding pattern until a Canadian court rejected an anti-nuclear group's attempt to block the test. At that point, the bomber with its unarmed Cruise missile began its 1500 mile run over Canada's frozen north, an area chosen because it is similar to Soviet terrain. The missiles were never fired, and the B-52 never landed in Canada. (CBS 3/6/84, :30)

The official dismissal of the test area as "Canada's frozen north" denies the existence of the political, cultural, and environmental vitality of Canada. Finally, the example reveals the importance of looking at the contexts in which meaning for foreign policy emerges. Domestic and international stories in combination develop meanings. Quantitative summaries of stories gathered simply because they mention Canada tend to overlook meaning that is generated by the organic form of domestic and foreign news elements in interaction.

The bulk of network television coverage of the cruise missile tests tends to be 10- or 20-second announcements with simple static graphics displayed behind the anchorman's reading. These matter-of-fact treatments gain political significance when considered in the context of the discourse of the audiences' political subcultures.

Brokow: A U.S. Cruise missile—that's an important factor in the Soviet-American nuclear equation—today an unarmed cruise missile crashed into the Beaufort sea soon after launch from a B-52 over Canada. Cause unknown. It was the sixth test of the missile and follows a similar failure last month. (NBC 2/25/86, :10)

The logic supports cruise testing as necessary and legitimate behavior in the context of "the Soviet–American nuclear equation." The innocuous way in which "equation" is offered as a definition of international reality against which certain actions are necessary represents the way the news can reinforce ideas about international relations for audiences not politically attuned to the specific issues so reported.

Similarly, the following report about a Canadian anti-cruise protest march includes a logic that can be interpreted as working against the political commitment and concern of anti-cruise forces. The suggestion that *light* rain deters political activism trivializes the political commitment of those involved. Again, the political orientation of the audience is key to such readings and in this case politically active viewers who are sympathetic to the protest are the ones likely to be offended by such reporting.

> Pictures: Aerial view of marchers crossing a bridge.

> Schiefer: The main demonstration in Vancouver fell short of expectations. 150,000 had been expected to march; light rain apparently kept the turnout much smaller. (CBS 2/25/85, :20)

Among networks, ABC is routinely the most detailed in its coverage of Canada.[23] In the case of the cruise missile tests, the ABC coverage is detailed in a linguistic and filmic sense and tends to be more politically provocative than the other networks. In the introduction to one such report, Peter Jennings takes care to ironically define Canada as a separate country:

> Jennings: Today, for the first time, an American cruise missile flew on its own over another country-the country is Canada-where on this day, as in the past, attitudes toward testing the cruise are very mixed. (ABC 2/19/85, 2:00)

The report juxtaposes Canadian versus American citizen perspectives by showing a short statement from each. First, a Canadian woman who is carrying her baby on her back as she speaks:

> Woman: I don't think the Americans have any business testing their missiles over Canadian space.

Response to her comment comes, first, in a shot of several men unfurling an American flag before the camera. Then a bearded American man wearing a jacket (clearly labeled U.S. Army) says:

> Man: (Paul Ocheltree) I think Canada has an obligation to participate in the development of weapon systems that may someday help preserve Canada.

This construction reveals political discourse that combines the news voice of Jennings and the film of the flag as competing, nationalistic referents in the context of the two recruited voices. It is invitational discourse. Jennings comments set the tone for the consideration of testing in light of Canadian sovereignty by reminding us that Canada is, after all, a separate country.

The television graphics in this piece dramatically represent the details of the test area lending specific features to the area that has in other reports been only an abstract space. These maps provide a much better under-standing of the test's relationship to recognizable features of Canadian geography than any of the static maps and descriptions in the print coverage. There are several animated representations of the actual flight path of the missiles during the test phase. And aerial footage from the perspective of the missile revealing a bird's eye view as the missile skims over the tops of Canadian forests, assumes a sinister tone when combined with an Air Force major's voice exclaiming the virtues of Canada in a way that feeds the press stereotype of Canada as a vast northern wasteland. "Canada provides snow covered terrain and a tremendous amount of space." The comment is especially ironic in light of Jennings' implicit appeal for us to recognize Canadian sovereignty.

There is little consensus in the political communications research about the policy implications of news coverage of protest activity. Some observers question the influence of domestic citizen groups' political action on foreign policy. Nossal, for example, in a review of the cruise missile test issue, concluded that the government averted attempts by peace groups to influence the policy because those groups did not present united preferences and, besides, he argued, electoral retribution on foreign policy issues is rare. He suggested that when opposition to a policy is intense the issue is often so regionalized that it creates local rather than national problems (p. 37).[24] Alternatively, if we are to account for the interaction of national and international responses to policy, it might be necessary to adopt a perspective that moves away from a closed-ended, either–or view of policymaking to one that reveals the long-term, incremental, dynamic nature of group influence on foreign policy. Reasons for adopting this perspective in order to better understand news treatment of the cruise issue include:

1. The examples analyzed here suggest that the peace groups' activity did influence the disposition of the tests, even though it did not stop them altogether. For example, Trudeau's remarks show a sensitivity to the opposition and the protests apparently influenced the decisions to halt the tests temporarily after the technical problems led to test failures.

2. Foreign policymakers rarely accommodate contemporary pressures for change in their active policies; they are more likely to try to change the public attitudes that challenge the policy. These rhetorical attempts to change public opinion are themselves a response to protests and reveal assumptions, and values that constitute the substance of policymaking.[25] The typical influence process involves a delayed response to protests. Recalling past expressions against policy, bureaucrats shape future policy so as to avoid what they perceive as negative, troublesome public response. It may, therefore, be premature to conclude that the cruise protests had no influence on policy, over the long term.

3. The protests were part of an international response, the final policy effect of which can only be understood by reviewing the larger international response and the political discourse that defined that response. Public internationalism is the province of bureaucrats, individual citizens and organized lobbying groups. The degree to which the discourse among them represents regional, national and transnational collaboration and shared responses to mutual interests deserves the close scrutiny of the international communication specialist.

Even though the protests did not stop the tests themselves, the rhetorical influence on policymaking was not spent at the moment of the first test flight. The culture of those opposed to such testing is likely to use the experience to enhance and refine its ongoing discourse for purposes of negotiating future policies. And the policymakers themselves, recalling the comparative force of the public discourse associated with past issues, will weigh its import in future decisions.

Unlike some, who believe that "society's ability to affect the process of foreign policy is quite limited" (p. 38),[26] Tucker is comparatively optimistic about transnational groups' influence and cites several examples of success.[27] Similarly, Griffiths advocated including unofficial rhetoric in international diplomacy, especially diplomacy involving arms control:

> Rather than continue to speak only in the language of the diplomatic and military-technical aspects of negotiation, Canadian representatives would also commence in effect to conduct a world propaganda in favour of transnational collaboration for arms limitation. (pp. 673–674)[28]

For Griffiths, the role of the public in transnational communications is essential:

> American and Soviet arms control advocates should . . . begin with an energetic effort to develop not only among themselves but also in the public-at-large a consciousness of transnational linkages and how they operate. (p. 671)[29]

SUMMARY

The domestic political cost, for Canada, of participating in the tests was not an issue in the American press over the entire 5-year period with the exception of one commentary piece in the print press mentioning that Canadian public opinion was opposed to the tests. Meanwhile, the Canadian press was alive with political discourse about the cruise issue. Significantly, for Canadian/American relations, Canadian domestic and Soviet international press accounts included a proposal from Gorbachev, made during a speech to the Canadian Parliament, for the United States and Soviets to halt the development of the cruise; an appeal that was not picked up by the American press reviewed.

The Canadian domestic political upheaval generated by the powerful, intercultural and internationally connected anti-cruise protest movement in which thousands of Canadians participated received only passing notice in the American press. When it was mentioned, American news editors tended to associate it with news about domestic crime. The occasional American newspaper "commentary," so labeled, provides much more detail about the Canadian citizen anti-cruise protests than the routine coverage. Conventional "hard news" formats tend to be opaque and reveal neither the rhetoric of the protests nor the political objectives of the protestors. The Soviet press reveals considerable detail about the protest activities by using the Canadian press as a primary source for this information.

Meanwhile, discussion of the costs of the test agreement to Canada's international diplomatic relationships was, except for the commentary piece noted, absent in the American press examined for the 5-year period. The agreement has implications for Canada's perceived sovereignty vis-à-vis Soviet/American relations. That is, the agreement might have been at the expense of Canadian diplomatic disaffection with the Soviets. Similarly, assessments of Canada's independence in the eyes of the larger international community might have changed as a result of the agreement. From an international perspective, the test agreement must be judged against Canada's established pattern of responding independently to certain Soviet initiatives. Despite the constant entreaties in the Soviet press for Canada not to agree to the tests, the Canadians did agree, and the image of Canadian foreign policy as reactive rather than independent was confirmed in this instance.

The Soviet press directs most of its hostility to the Americans in covering the cruise testing. Although the Canadian and Soviet press prominently displayed the argument that the Canadians were being co-opted by the United States in agreeing to the tests, the press examples reveal the hypocrisy of that stance on the part of the Canadians by reminding the world of Trudeau's nuclear "suffocation" speech at the U.N. and by reporting how intimately the Canadians had become involved in the tests as military–technical operatives and as press and public relations spokespersons. The main issue, from our perspective, is that the American press, by failing to include the Soviet charge of cooption, a charge also routinely made by protestors in the Canadian press, denied the American news consumer important information through which he or she might have more accurately guaged Canada's international political credibility, and judged the significance of this apparently hypocritical decision within the larger context of Canadian/American affairs. Similarly, the American press denied the politically active Canadian/American watcher the opportunity to make informed judgments about the test policy by failing to report the Soviet international rhetoric linking the tests with American environmental abuses, with concurrent NATO military exercises held in Canada, U.S./Canadian trade agreements, and America's poor safety record in such tests. Across the news examples, only the Soviet press raised the first-strike issue even though U.S. non-press sources reveal that it was a topic of considerable concern among American strategists themselves.

NOTES

1. Atwood, M. (1968). From the poem "Backdrop Addresses Cowboy." In *The Animals in That Country*. Boston: Little, Brown.

2. Planning U.S. Strategic Nuclear Forces for the 1980's. (1979). Budget Issue Paper for Fiscal Year 1979, Congressional Budget Office, Congress of the United States, Washington, DC: U.S. Government Printing Office.

3. Betts, R. K. (1982). *Cruise missiles and U.S. policy*. Washington, DC: The Brookings Institution.

4. Gordon, M. (1984, June 6). Trudeau's legacy. *National Journal* p. 1231.

5. Gordon, Op. Cit.

6. This definition of sovereignty is from Holsti, K. J. *International Politics,* Op. Cit., pp. 79–80.

7. Caldwell, L. K. Binational responsibilities for a shared environment. In C. F. Doran & J. Sigler (Eds.), *Canada and the United States,* Op. Cit., p. 209.

8. Holmes, J. Op. Cit., p. 84.

9. Clarkson, S. (1982). *Canada and the Reagan challenge*. Toronto: James Lorimer.

10. Holmes, J. Op. Cit., p. 234.

11. Munton, D. (1978). Stimulus–response and continuity in Canadian foreign policy behavior during Cold War and detente. In B. Tomlin (Ed.), *Canada's foreign policy: Analysis and trends*. Toronto: Methuen.

12. Raymond, G. (1987). Canada between the superpowers: Reciprocity and conformity in foreign policy. *The American Review of Canadian Studies, 17*(2), 221–236.

13. As mentioned earlier, the typical pattern of international press reportage begins with an event, such as a formal treaty signing, visiting dignitaries, and so on, followed by the introduction of related issues and arguments generated by participants and the press. However, for several reasons, an unnecessary restriction is placed on the data when it is squeezed into symmetrical event–issue–argument sets. First, issues are sometimes raised by politically active people and reported by the press in the absence of apparent "newsworthy" events. Second, each of the dimensions in the event–issue–argument set has an implicit rhetorical force of its

own. For example, any news discourse reporting an event has the force of argument by virtue of selectivity and the shaping effects of standard news conventions. Finally, an event is often reported in the absence of a recognized political issue or argument; that is, the event may not have been sufficiently assimilated into the realm of political analysis and discourse to register in journalistic accounts as issues or formal arguments. Therefore, in order to best represent the dynamics of press discourse, the examples of events, issues, and arguments are listed as they occurred in the sample in roughly chronological order whether or not they are represented by all elements of the expected "set" of three variables.

14. Betts, Op. Cit.

15. Gwynn, R. Op. Cit., p. 128.

16. The Fellowship of Reconciliation was founded in 1915 and claims to have 32,000 members comprised of "religious pacifists drawn from all faiths, including over 4,000 clergy and many teachers, professors and professional workers. (The fellowship) attempts, through education and action, to substitute nonviolence and reconciliation for violence in international relations, racial and intergroup tensions and other tension spots" (p. 1443). Encyclopedia of Associations, 23rd edition, Gale Research Inc., 1989.

17. A number of studies have pointed to the nonreciprocal nature of news sharing between Canada and the United States. See, for example the citations in note 16 in the introduction to this book. The Canadian Press news agency is shown in these studies to be primarily a repository for American news interpretations, and Canadian news generated by that service is rarely picked up by the more powerful and dominating American wire services. See for example, Thompson, D. C. (1978). *The coverage of Canada in the U.S. news media: A study of inadequacy.* Unpublished Master's thesis, Carlton University, Ottawa, Ontario, Canada.

18. The Canadian government's formal environmental assessment reviewed the potential impact of the tests in five categories: (a) Release of effluents from the cruise missile and support aircraft, (b) noise produced by the missile and support aircraft at ground level, (c) the risk of collision between the missile in normal flight and low-flying aircraft, (d) the risk of population and other environmental considerations from impacting debris or fire from a failed missile, and (c) socioeconomic effects on CFB Cold Lake and surrounding areas. Although the report concluded that there would be no significant or adverse environmental impact on the Canadian test corridor, it admitted that the noise would have some effect on wildlife, and that sociopolitical issues associated with the tests remain unresolved. This is an important exclusion in light of arguments by some protestors that assurances of minimum safety risks are made on the basis of low population density. Such assurances, they argue, constitute an arrogant attitude toward the native peoples, small though their numbers may be, who inhabit the regions along the test corridor. See An Initial Environmental Evaluation on the Proposal to Conduct Air Launched Cruise Missile Flight Tests in the Canadian Test Corridor. (1983, September 30). The Directorate of Military Plans and Operations, National Defense Headquarters, Ottawa.

19. Pfaltzgraff, R. L. Jr., & Davis, J. K. (1977). *The cruise missile: Bargaining chip or defense bargain?* Washington DC: Corporate Press.

20. Problems with Northrops cruise guidance system became a public issue again

in 1989. See, for example, Associated Press Report, "Justice Department Joins Northrop Lawsuit" 3/11/89. This news item reports that

it is alleged Northrop's Western Services Department in El Monte systematically falsified test data, failed to perform certain tests and manipulated test equipment to obtain false results on the guidance system of the nuclear warhead missile.

21. For a discussion of the concept of "The Identification of the Enemy in Riot Myths" see Edelman, 1971, Op. Cit., p. 109.

22. Hall, S. (1974). Deviance, politics and the media. In Rock, P. & M. McIntosh (Eds.), *Deviance and social control* (pp. 261–305). London: Tavistock.

23. In an extended interview, one executive news producer from another American television network informed me that Jennings is recognized in the industry as being internationally tuned and organizing his newscasts accordingly. This producer also said that in contrast to ABC, his particular network intentionally follows American foreign policy as a guide to what is internationally relevant. This news strategy has obvious implications for the extent to which television news might offer alternatives to and arguments about American policy from international voices.

24. Nossal, K. R. (1985). *The politics of Canadian foreign policy.* Scarborough, Ontario: Prentice-Hall.

25. Davison, 1976, Op. Cit., p. 397.

26. Nossal, Op. Cit., p. 38.

27. Tucker, Op. Cit., pp. 16–22; 33–101.

28. Griffiths, Op. Cit., pp. 673–674.

29. Griffiths, Op. Cit., p. 671.

Chapter 7

Free Trade: Dealing in Cultural Futures

It is only when we listen to those *being eaten,* eaten alive, that the essence of the empire is revealed: *consumption.*

— B. Livant (p. 27)[1]

It is, perhaps, fortunate that the debate over free trade has brought into full view the homely and cacaphonous nature of both the Canadian and American varieties of nationalistic rhetoric. Rarely has an issue allowed us the opportunity to so fully appreciate the stark reality of the nationalism that has over the years worked, often beyond public preview, to shape and to generally constrain reciprocal public discourse. It is unfortunate, however, that the debate continues to be reported in isolated halves by two separate, monophonic North American voices. The American press serves up the pro-American view, whereas the Canadian press coverage of its national debate barely penetrates the American border. The presumed importance of free trade for the economic survival of both countries brought forth the old jingoistic skeletons, each regaled in its full dress of cultural symbology. The participants include pro-culturalists, proponents of cultural sovereignty, Canadian free-traders, anti-nationalists, and latter-day apologists for American manifest destiny. Nationalistic rhetoric in the heat of the free-trade debate abandons diplomatic facades. Most of the language provides a stark contrast to the customary platitudes and cliches of "good neighbors," "world's largest trading partners," the "special relationship," and the "world's longest undefended border." The evolving discourse has become an ongoing marathon debate that includes entreaties, threats, apologies and self-fulfilling financial and cultural analyses.

The debate within Canada between the pro-Canadian culturalists and the Canadian free-traders indicates how the convergence of politics and culture can dominate the national discourse that informs the policy of international relations. Because this particular issue is significantly salient for the publics of both countries (unlike acid rain, which has been more a Canadian preoccupation) it provides a useful comparative opportunity to understand how the American press, compared to the Canadian press, appears to be accommodating Canada's most intense public political debate about America's threat to its culture. Here is an example of a politically active Canadian subculture engaged in a public rhetorical campaign denouncing free trade as a threat to national sovereignty, and a larger Canadian public participating in profound cultural introspection before, begrudgingly, agreeing to open itself fully to American commerce. An examination of examples of press coverage of free trade promises to reveal whether, in this instance, the news as a market driven commodity reflects only economic dimensions of the argument, or, alternatively, constitutes a relatively independent source of information sensitive to the complex interaction of culture, politics and economic forces.

BACKGROUND

In January 1989, President Reagan and Canadian Prime Minister Brian Mulroney signed a free-trade accord. The agreement represents a desire to enhance further the mutual economic advantages that have accrued from Canada and the United States having become the world's largest trading partners. For the most part, the prospect of a free-trade agreement generated overwhelming approval in America, but it was one of the most hotly debated international political issues in Canadian history. Canadians' long-smoldering fears of American cultural imperialism were fanned into a firestorm by the trade issue. Brian Mulroney cast his political fate in support of the free trade bill and his ultimately successful re-election campaign served as the stage for a dramatic national referendum on free trade. John Turner and his Liberal Party termed the trade deal the "sale of Canada Act." Ed Broadbent's leftist opposition New Democrats had threatened to tear up the trade bill. On Monday, November 21, 1988, Mulroney's Progressive Conservative Party won a decisive parliamentary majority in one of the most bitter political campaigns in Canada's 121-year history. His victory assured that Canadians would, after all, support the free-trade agreement. Mulroney could hardly subdue his contempt for the proculturalists whose appeals to anti-Americanism had, at one point, nearly cost him the election. Mulroney's remarks, in a post-election speech, show the scars earned in the pitched battle between pro versus anti-free traders in Canada.

> Americans might reflect on the fact that there is in Canada as in other industrialized countries a well of anti-Americanism. It happens that it's not enough to elect a dog-catcher, but this doesn't stop people from trying to whip it up. I've already indicated what I think of this kind of activity, and I think the Canadian people have indicated what they think of it too. (p. A.12)[2]

However, undaunted, anti free-trade forces in Canada promised to continue the fight. One example is the Pro-Canada Network, a coalition of 20 national organizations including church groups, environmentalists, and women's groups. The Network was established in 1987 for the specific purpose of battling the trade agreement. Their rhetoric during the campaign centered on the potential impact free trade would have on Canada's network of health and social programs.

The trade agreement proposes to remove all tariffs and restrictions in Canadian/American trade for the next 10 years. Economists believe that when the agreement is fully operational after 10 years, Canada's economy will expand 5% faster than it would otherwise. For Canadians, the accord offers an American market of 270 million; the Canadian domestic market is a comparatively paltry 26 million. The American economy is expected to grow one percent faster as a direct result of the deal.[3] The free-trade bill seemed to be consistent with the general trend in Europe; the 12 nations of the European Community were planning to drop all internal trade barriers by the end of 1992. The accord was seen by some observers as the first essential step in the emergence of a North American trading system that is likely to include Mexico, having the potential to handily outperform the European common market. Two weeks following the Canadian elections, Canada was host to the trade ministers of 96 nations, in a General Agreement on Tariffs and Trade (GATT) meeting in Montreal as part of what is called the "Uruguay Round" talks that were to conclude in 1990. In many ways the Canadian/American free-trade pact was to serve as a model for the Uruguay Round. One of the major items on that group's agenda included proposals to reduce barriers to trade among the participating nations.

Why, then, were certain Canadian activists flying in the face of what seems to be a rational course for these North American partners and a world-wide trend toward international trade arrangements?

Predictably, the bell-ringers for free trade, early on, in the United States were the Reagan Administration and its perennial power base, the major American corporations. Reagan and Mulroney had decided to aggressively pursue the trade agreement at their "Shamrock Summit" meeting on St.

Patrick's Day in 1985. The Canadians came up with the idea in the first place in the midst of their concerns that the Americans were likely to become more protectionist in their international trade policy, thereby shutting Canada out of this lucrative market. Canadian tariffs on such commodities as wood products had long been a sore point for U.S. corporations. Along with other trade protectionist policies, these tariffs contributed to the antagonistic pall that defined Canadian/American relations, especially in the Trudeau/Reagan years. The Canadian business and financial community spent millions of dollars on an advertising campaign boosting the free-trade agreement. Canadian opponents argued that free trade would inevitably exacerbate existing imbalances between the two countries. Canadians would lose jobs they argued, whereas American multinationals would run roughshod through the Canadian economy forcing Canadian industry into unacceptable compromises in order to survive. There appeared, at first glance, to be no serious American opposition to the pact.[4]

THE EMERGING FORM OF PRESS COVERAGE

The most intense and provocative debate among Canadians generated by the free-trade issue was and continues to be centered on the likely impact of free trade on Canadian cultural identity. Indeed some observers concluded that Quebec was the strongest supporter of free trade because, as the French-speaking province, it is secure in its cultural identity and sees no threat from American culture.[5] Others, revealing further the complexity of the interaction of politics and culture, noted that after the bill's passage certain Quebec politicians' praised the agreement for its power to break up the country and further Quebec sovereignty.[6]

Fueling the debate is the seemingly paranoic fervor of the Canadian pro-culturalists, sometimes referred to as *cultural pessimists* (p. 105)[7] They constitute an activist, elite political subculture in their own right. Their public language is seen by some as refreshing and articulate political discourse; by others as lock-stepped, selfish rhetoric based in nationalistic appeals that seem strangely contradictory to the values expected from the community of intellectuals and artists. The free-trade issue both before and since its passage has provided a new and intense forum for this political subculture.

Of course the public, political discourse of intellectuals has been, historically, a controversial phenomenon in North America. The tension is most often located between conservative and liberal interpretations of nationalistic ideologies and the proper role of intellectualism in society.

From the Dreyfus affair to the Vietnam War, conservatives howled that intellectuals meddled in matters outside their training. (p. 199)[8]

Alternatively, the liberal intellectuals bemoan the inevitable corruption of their peers occasioned by publicity and economic success. The market, in effect, compromises the intensity of their social corrective discourse. C. Wright Mills, for example, complained that

instead of criticizing the mediocrity and mindlessness, they savor their new status; instead of acting as the "moral conscience of society," they confound prosperity with advancing culture. (p. 79)[9]

Many Canadian intellectuals, even after the formal approval of free trade, refuse to consent to the proposed ideal of an open marketplace. At the heart of their concern is an understanding of the power of language and symbols; of the primacy of communication for a culture's autonomy. This is a familiar public preoccupation in bilingual Canada. Of special concern to Canadian proculturists is the institution of subsidies, grants, and other protectionist policies undertaken over the years by the Canadian government to protect Canada's culture industries, those industries in which the language of Canadian culture resides. (These industries are generally understood to include publishing, music, art, literature, media performance, and production, etc.) Even though the trade agreement includes a clause that exempts the Canadian cultural industries a qualifier in the clause raises fears that short-term grandfathering protection will gradually fade away. The qualifier suggests that:

notwithstanding any other provision of this agreement either of the parties has the right to take retaliatory measures in response to actions that would have been inconsistent with this agreement. (p. 7)[10]

Will the subsidies be bargained away under such provisions? Even worse, the culturalists wonder, will the avalanche of cross-border commerce bury the concern for cultural protection altogether? Will the United States engage in retaliations if it believes that certain government grants to book publishers, for example, were not made available to the subsidiaries of that publisher in the United States? A Canadian journalist recalls the very real history of American financial retaliations:

Free trade proponents note that the United States retaliated in the past when Ottawa prevented Canadian companies from claiming advertising time bought on U.S. border television stations as tax-deductible expenses. The United States complained for years, but ultimately introduced similar legislation that restricts the ability of U.S. companies to claim tax deductions for advertising time bought on Canadian border TV stations.

The terms of the trade deal, free trade supporters say, merely formalize the retaliation process that is already in effect. (p. D3)[11]

The Canadian press reveals that many Canadians fear their culture is being swallowed by the American empire despite years of concocting complex, often bizarre strategies to avoid that possibility.

After the Free Trade Bill was approved Canadian author Margaret Atwood, the stinging nettle of Canadian culturalists, in her characteristically terse and prickly manner, remarked that

the kind of people (who voted for the agreement) know very little about the connection between what we genially refer to as culture and what we genially refer to as politics. They think culture is a bunch of people jumping around in long underwear. (p. 7)[12]

The free-trade debate put to the test the Canadians' ability to articulate what is meant by Canadian versus American culture. Economist John Kenneth Galbraith, a Canadian, represents the middle-road between the opposing parties in the debate—the business and artistic communities. Galbraith believes that Canadian identity is expressed in neither economics nor the arts but in public administration. He concluded that Canada is, on balance, better governed than the United States. Consequently, having an abiding faith in "any Canadian government worthy of the office," Galbraith remains "deeply unimpressed by Canadian concern over subjugation to American corporate power" because such a government can keep American multinationals in their proper place in Canada.[13]

Fil Fraser, a Canadian Black, isolates Canada's identity in its successful transition from "a deeply (though subtly) racist society into a country that's multiracial, multicultural, and so astonishingly diverse it ought to be the envy of the world" (p. 180).[14]

Adrienne Clarkson, Ontario's agent-general in Paris, defined the perennial Canadian identity dilemma as an international–intercultural communication problem. She believes that Canadians have plenty of identity; the problem lies in their not being able to "show it to other people" (p. 98).[15] She implied that Canada's transnational voice proclaiming its distinctiveness among nations is being repressed.

Canadian Andrew Coyne, some 6 months after the election, reflected on Canadian public discussion about the free-trade issue, and assailed the Canadian preoccupation with national identity. His essay appeared in Canada's *Saturday Night Magazine*.

the identity fixation has given nationalism a bad name. Far from generating a sense of ourselves as US, it has promoted alienation and self-doubt. The policies it has entailed-substituting the bloodless creed of statism for the free will of individuals-have drained all vitality from our consciousness of nation-hood. (p. 26)[16]

He described the identity fixation as a self-serving, hegemonic tool of the Canadian elite.

the first reflex of Canadian nationalism is *exclusivism,* the attempt to block out alien (read American) influences via controls on the import of foreign goods, capital, people, and ideals . . . Exclusivism and statism are the tools of elites, just as they are also the means of their rise and preservation. And the imperative of identity gives them their cause: thus the assumption of a guiding role in defining the nation by powerful coteries in government, business, labour and the media.

He attempted to construct a tragic irony behind the culturalists' debate:

Far from safeguarding our independence, Canadian nationalism has made us almost wholly psychologically dependent on the U.S., mixing equal parts envy of American achievement, fear of American influence, and smug contempt for American values, real or imagined, but always measuring, for good or ill, by the American example. Only when we discard all attempts to promote a separate identity will we finally declare our independence.

Coynes apparently worked from an implicit belief in a liberal internation-alist perspective, an idealized world where all nations and their cultures, regardless of size, GNP, military strength, or degree of access to and representation in the international press are equal players in the interna-tional forum.

This is not a belief shared by Canadian author and journalist Robertson Davies. Writing in the American magazine *Harper's,* Davies urged caution in dealing with the Americans. Davies recalled several violations of trust to qualify his reluctance to support free trade.

The immediate American response has been that the United States has no intention of taking over its northern neighbor. But—and here I must write with the utmost tact—the gap between profession and practice is no less in U.S. foreign policy than it has been in that of any other great power when dealing with a smaller one. While expressing respect for our national sovereignty, U.S. submarines, uninvited, are in our Arctic waters and won't go away. American banks have sought to establish themselves in Canada without regard for our own banking system. We watch with dismay the cavalier treatment the United States gives to international agreements when these agreements do not suit American policy. (p. 44)[17]

Davies eschewed the term *national culture* "because it has been abused by people who think of culture as a commodity, separable from the rest of national life." Instead, he believes that "culture is an ambience, a part of the air we breathe." He identified a distinctive Canadian political culture worth protecting from the unchecked marketplace:

> What virtually all Americans, and too many Canadians who deal in the international world of money, fail utterly to understand is that Canada is that political oddity—a socialist monarchy. We have created an elaborate and very successful welfare state under a monarchical setup, which is itself a declaration that there are things of national importance that are above politics and above simple matters of finance.

Davies, like many others in the Canadian intellectual community, is genuinely fearful of the impact of free trade on his culture and expresses disappointment in the judgment of his fellow citizens in supporting free trade.

> Political unity with a more aggressive and powerful country may not mean the death of the essence of one's own country. But such a link could be dangerous and in some respects depleting, and I wish the majority of Canadians had had the good sense to declare against it. A strong link already exists, and it is sufficient without turning the link into a shackle.

With the exception of the Davies essay, the American press shared with the American public only brief glimpses of this Canadian national debate. Beyond this isolated example of a Canadian's perspective given center stage in a leading prestige magazine, the American press coverage of the free-trade issue reveals several recurring patterns; the presentation of Canada as comparatively unsophisticated in the game of international economics, and a clear account of the sheer aggression the Americans were bringing to the free-trade bargaining table, including threats to the Canadians that relations would deteriorate if they failed to approve the pact. Some of the American press reports centered on the suspicious nature of Canadians as one explanation for their internal squabble over passing the bill:

> Canadians can be a suspicious people, especially when it comes to the United States, which has twice invaded this land. The fact that the Senate overwhelmingly and quickly ratified the trade treaty is not seen here (in Canada)

as positive but rather as convincing evidence that Canada somehow got a raw deal. (p. 18)[18]

Even selected Canadian commentary reported in the American press stress their suspicions and fears. Ken Dryden, a Canadian government lawyer assigned to study the treaty remarked before its passage that:

> There is a very deep-seated feeling in the pit of every Canadian's stomach. This feeling is an anxiety that when you live beside a place as big as the United States, no matter how much you may like or admire it, you must keep it at arm's length lest you eventually be consumed by your friend. A handshake is one thing. A hug is another. (p. 18)[19]

Canadian Professor James Careless accounted for the Canadian character as an interaction of historical adaptation to climate and social–political forces:

> Americans cannot conceive of losing unless there's a conspiracy somewhere. Canadians, constrained by climate, distance and history, see no reason to expect victory. (p. 18)

Less typical is this reference in the same report to Canadian Author Peter Newman's more optimistic assessment of Canada's evolution:

> After feeling for more than a century that being Canadian was a journey rather than a destination, we have arrived at last. We have attained a delicious grace which allows us to appreciate that what's important is not so much who we are but what we are.

The bulk of the reports in the Canadian press reveal that the Canadian proculturalists are suspicious of deals that encourage an overreliance on market forces. Their rhetoric is poised to question the impact of unrestricted economic forces on their essential communication processes. For Canadians, these communication practices are built into the intertwined promises of peace, order, good government; a distinct national identity and the cultural mosaic. These dissenting Canadians share the intellectual posture of the international community of cultural pessimists who, in their most extreme vision, see

> no reason to expect anything from technological developments than an acceleration of trends they already deplore . . . especially a continuation of the shift away from involving people in society as political citizens of nation states toward involving them as consumption units in a corporate world. (p. 105)[20]

From a political communications perspective, the question raised by the Canadian proculturalists and reported primarily in the Canadian (not the American) press is what, if any, new opportunities for public, participatory political discourse, especially among Canadians, are served up by the deal? This is a question that directly involves the future of the Canadian mass media systems and their contents as carriers of the lifeblood of Canadian culture. The history of Canadian public media and the arts reveals that both have been developed and sustained with passing regard to profit margins for the purpose of protecting the Canadian culture from the menace to the south. They are the essential components of Canadian identity; the forum and substance of the discourse about what it means to be Canadian. The trade deal is the hobgoblin threatening the demise of that cultural incubator. Unbridled international consumption, the proculturalists argue, will replace the communications through which Canadians display their cultural wares, engage in a shared dialogue and by consensus agree about who they are and who they want to become.

There is considerable support for this argument from non-Canadians in the international community who believe that global market forces constrain a nation's political participation in a deceptive way by substituting an array of temporary consumption opportunities, including new communication hardware, in place of more substantive discourse.

> The slight of hand lies in the assumption that new technologies will increase general access to information and open up new possibilities of two-way communications. (p. 2)[21]

This view sees the global market as a machine that homogenizes cultures by flattening arguments, discouraging partisanship, and reducing public discourse to debates about which products to buy, which media stars to admire, which fashions and trends to mimic. The politics convenient to the market forces go unchallenged. The trade deal, under this interpretation, threatens the last bastion of partisan public discourse, public broadcasting, by commercializing communications in a way that will, intentionally or not, serve to support the vision of the global marketeers.

The Canadian communication nightmare is that American-based diverse programming, attractively although deceptively packaged as personally relevant consumer goods, will be made available through an even wider array of communication technologies. The public audience will thereby become fractured; the Canadians' town meeting tent will be folded and put away due to lack of attendance, and the discourse for building Canadian identity will fall silent. Elliot sees this kind of process as a threat to the public broadcasting systems of all nations, not just Canada's and describes the progression as follows:

The pressure will be felt in two ways. First, the new distributive forms will simply leave out political discussion and criticism. Actuality programming, topical, with limited appeal, is the type of content most at risk. Second, the development of new distributive systems puts public broadcasting under severe threat. (p. 112)[22]

Clarkson's analysis of the impact of the Reagan Administration on Canada seems to recognize the progression:

The severe cuts to the budget of the Canadian Broadcasting Corporation and other crucial cultural institutions in November 1984 gave a triple message as a blow against public television, a rebuff to the liberal media establishment and a declaration of faith in the free, necessarily continental market for culture. (p. 368)[23]

Schiller addresses the likely impact market forces will have on the very language of public discourse as it now exists on public communications systems. His predictions are dire:

Rational citizens are the last thing on earth that corporate advertizers seek. It is no accident that structures of public service broadcasting and culture are their primary targets scheduled for demolition. (p. 323)[24]

Indeed, if accurate, this prediction also has implications for reducing further the tiny amount of detailed coverage of Canada that reaches Americans via American public broadcasting. National Public Radio, subsidized as it is by a grant from the Donner Foundation, routinely covers Canadian affairs. And, the most detailed representation of the free trade and culture debate among Canadians prior to their election was presented on the McNeal–Lehrer program, on American Public Television.[25]

By extension, the logic of these cultural pessimists suggests that rather than encouraging transnational discourse among citizens of the two countries, an ultimately unassailable international corporate voice will emerge as the prevailing force in our transborder public communications as a result of the trade agreement. The language of Canada's culture will be replaced by self-serving corporate discourse:

Corporate speech . . . is indistinguishable from corporate global activity. Accordingly challenges to this "speech" are regarded as violations of freedom. Specifically, it is the corporations' freedom to receive and transmit messages anywhere, anytime. (p. 327)[26]

Canadian J. David McLaren, writing in the Toronto Globe and Mail, helps us understand the distinctions between international corporate voices and the weaker, more subtle, interconnected cultural voices of a nation as they compete for a platform in international discourse.

> The voice of a nation is heard in its art, and film, and television. The products of television and film should not be confused with art because rarely do they achieve that end. But neither should they be omitted from a discussion on culture, for they are powerful culture bearers. (p. D6)[27]

Mindful of the threat of the American film and broadcasting presence, he sketches the features of a media tradition unknown to most Americans:

> Our own voice is not as strident as that of the Americans and it is more particular than that of the British. It is the voice of a certain small boy growing up in a certain small prairie town in *Who Has Seen The Wind*. It is the quiet complaint of a particular woman victimized by the barren, typically Hogtown world, in *Life Before Man*. . . . Some have called our voice puny and provincial. Perhaps it is (but) . . . we could not escape our provincialism even if we wanted to.

McLaren concluded that "Perhaps the Canadian voice simply cannot be heard above the din of the American product." And, like Davies, saw free trade as an eroding menace, slowly strangling the Canadian cultural voice:

> We do have a voice of our own. It emerges out of a singular way of looking at the world that owes nothing to the cultures of either the Americans or the British. But we are in danger of losing it entirely, and with it any sense of ourselves as a sovereign nation, unique in the world and able to determine the shape of our own society.

The American press has no satisfactory answer to the question of whether free trade indeed threatens to replace Canada's "puny and provincial" cultural voices with an American-based multinational corporate growl. It does not address the question at all. On the other hand, there are recurring reports of the arguments for free trade. These reports disclose the second major pattern in the American press coverage of free trade; aggressive, threatening arguments for free trade on the part of the Americans. For example, there was mounting diplomatic pressures on Mulroney to convince Canadians to support the bill. Clyde Farnsworth reported in the New York Times of November 9, 1988 that

> Rufus Yerxa, staff director of the House Ways and Means trade subcommittee, said: "The Canadians cannot expect things to remain calm and passive if this agreement goes down in flames. It's going to have repercussions for the trading relationship." He insisted that "we won't be looking for ways to

penalize Canada, but we will be a lot less inclined to find ways of accommodating them in certain problems that we have." (pp. D5.6)[28]

Much to the dismay of Canadian proculturalists, Mulroney picked up on
the American quid-pro-quo argument in his campaign speeches, suggesting
that no real progress could be made on acid rain if free trade went down to
defeat. Free trade as an essential Canadian bargaining chip in American
relations was a major appeal in the campaign from Canadian and American
economists summarizing this position as follows:

> There will always be problems in a relationship so vast and complex as this
> one. "But if the trade pact goes down to defeat," he said, "we will certainly be
> entering into a dangerous phase." He added, "There are problems that can
> grow in difficulty." (p. D6)[29]

Although the American press was not interested in revealing the details of
the Canadian anti-American proculturist arguments, it was even less willing
to provide insight into the Canadian domestic political milleau in which that
debate occurred. Regional political–cultural issues are inseparable subsets
of National Canadian cultural protection, and the rhetoric and objectives of
the advocates from these camps often work at cross purposes. The
anti-American proculturalists argument, based as it is in Ontario, cannot be
understood apart from the regional diversity debate. For within Canada,
the Free Trade Bill became a rallying point for Western Canadian prov-
inces. Some of their citizens see the free-trade deal as a liberating force from
their long economic and cultural domination by central Canada. To them,
the proculturist Canadian opposition was more representative of a small
Ontario elite than of Canada as a whole. For example, Ontario Industry
Minister Monte Kwinter criticized the Free Trade deal by concluding that "if
it's a bad deal for Ontario, by extension it's a bad deal for Canada." David
Kilgour, M.P. from Strathcona, Alberta who supports free trade replied:

> His (Kwinter's) quip indicated that little had changed in a century-old attitude
> held by many Ontarians that what is good for them is also good for Canada
> as a whole. How can Canadian federalism preserve and protect regional
> interests and unite Canadians everywhere, if it is constantly undermined by
> the assertion that what suits one province suits all? (p. 91)[30]

For the most part, the American press plotted an all-is-well narrative after
the approval of the deal, an attitude that encourages us to ignore any
lingering cultural–imperialism artifacts kicking around from the debate
about free trade. Canadian officials and the Canadian press are now
presented as contrite economic realists.

> While Canadian officials can and do talk tough behind closed doors, they seem less inclined now to air grievances in Canada's nationalistic press, always eager to spot David vs. Goliath confrontations. . . . The new attitude, also reflected in the election results, was in marked contrast to the kind of poor cousin resentment and inferiority complex that long characterized the attitudes of many Canadians when they thought about the United States. (p. 2)[31]

Only a remnant of the Canadian nationalistic beast remains, in the form of Pierre Sarrazin:

> a Director who is writing a satirical movie script about a war between adjoining American and Canadian towns. "In Canada we stress the tribe more, not your rampant individualism. We finance a huge social security net; yours is more every-man-for-himself."

But Sarrazin's comments, are cast in this report as nothing more than the last, sour-grape gasps of the cultural pessimists. For after all, the journalist reveals, the free trade deal has a built in "dispute resolution process," and one senior American diplomat assures us that ". . . with the Canadians, the assumption always is that something can be worked out" (p. 2).[32]

Absent from the American press during the free-trade discussions was the occasional self-deprecating commentary that helps put current political expediencies into perspective while inviting resolution of the hostilities that have emerged in the heat of policymaking. David Broder's commentary from 1983 is an example of the type of discourse that can make a positive contribution to the American reader's comprehension of the present debate.

> We are the 800-pound gorilla in this hemisphere and, more often than not, we have acted it. We ought to bear that in mind when we decide that we have the wisdom to decide the future of some smaller country to whom the Lord has shown special favor by allowing it to live in the shadow of the United States.
>
> The picture of Lyndon Johnson strangling Lester Pearson at Camp David is not one that clamours to be a model of what we like to call our "good neighbor" policy. (p. B7)[33]

Their cause, barely acknowledged in the bulk of the American press, the Canadian cultural pessimists are left to resurrect and reconsider the strategy uttered by Sandra Gotlieb some years ago to a New York Times reporter. It is a strategy that acknowledges the dual preoccupations of the press towards drama and pro-nationalism.

> For some reason, a glaze passes over people's faces when you say Canada. Maybe we should invade South Dakota or something. (p. B7)[34]

The free-trade deal promises to reaffirm the power of existing arrangements in the American media empire rather than reshape them into a system that is responsive to a plurality of North American cultures. The press reports about free trade serve as one indicator, perhaps the leading edge, of that market-driven process. This review of the emerging form of American press coverage of free trade reveals that little more than a few snippets of the color, energy, and substance of Canada's ongoing national political debate are shared with Americans. There is no indication that this pattern of coverage is likely to change. These forms rehearse American power, exclude intercultural details, and offer no clear invitations to a more reciprocal Canadian/American dialogue.

NOTES

1. Livant, B. (1989). The imperial cannibal. In I. Angus & S. Jhally (Eds.), *Cultural politics in contemporary America* (pp. 26–36). New York: Routledge.

2. Mulroney to push approval of U.S.-Canadian pact. (1988, November 23). *New York Times,* p. A12.

3. U.S.–Canada pact implies big change for world trade. (1988, November 23). *New York Times,* p. A12.

4. Exceptions to consensus support for the agreement among the American business community include some mining, energy groups concerned about Canadian competition in these areas. See for example *New York Times,* 11/9/88, p. 1.

5. Mulroney faces fight to survive. (1988, November 18). *The Associated Press,* p. 1.

6. A new push for Quebec's independence. (1988, December 4). *New York Times,* p. 16.

7. Elliott, P. (1986). Intellectuals, the information society and the disappearance of the public sphere. In R. Collins, J. Curran, N. Garnham, P. Scannell, P. Schlesinger, & C. Sparks (Eds.), *Media, culture and society: A critical reader* (pp. 105–115). London: Sage.

8. Jacoby, R. (1987). *The last intellectuals.* New York: Noonday.

9. This interpretation of Mills is from Jacoby, Op. Cit., p. 79.

10. Canada's arts community still fears U.S. cultural imperialism. (1989, July 3–9). *The Washington Post National Weekly Edition,* p. 7.

11. A nagging question: Is Canadian culture in or out?. (1988, November, 12). *Toronto Globe and Mail,* p. D3.

12. Canada's arts community still fears U.S. cultural imperialism. (1989, July 3–9). *Washington Post National Weekly Edition,* p. 7

13. Galbraith, J. K. (1987, January). Canada customs. *Saturday Night,* pp. 113–118.

14. Fraser, F. (1987, January). Black like me. *Saturday Night,* pp. 180–184.

15. Clarkson, A. (1987, January). Over Home. *Saturday Night,* pp. 93–100.

16. Coyne, A. (1989, July). Let this be the last essay on the Canadian identity. *Saturday Night,* pp. 22–30.

17. Davies, R. (1989, January). Signing away Canada's soul: Culture, identity and the free trade agreement. *Harper's,* pp. 43–47.

18. Canada's deeper identity NOT made in the U.S.A. (1988, November 20). *New York Times,* p. 18.

19. Ibid.

20. Elliott, Op. Cit.

21. Nora, S. & Minc, A. (1978). *L'Information de la Societe* [The information society]. Paris: La Documentation Francaise.

22. Elliott, Op. Cit., p. 112.

23. Clarkson, S. (1985). *Canada and the Reagan challenge.* Toronto: Lorimer.

24. Schiller, H. (1989). The privatization of culture. In I. Angus & S. Jhally (Eds.), *Cultural politics in contemporary America* (pp. 317–332). New York: Routledge.

25. See, for example, Hodding Carter's report on the Cultural Implications of Free Trade, October, 1988.

26. Schiller, Op. Cit., p. 327.

27. McLaren, D. M. (1987, April 25). A voice to be preserved. *Toronto Globe and Mail,* p. D6.

28. *New York Times,* 11/9/88.

29. Ibid.

30. Kilgour, D. (1988). *Uneasy patriots.* Edmunton: Lone Pine Publishing.

31. Renegotiating a North American friendship. (1988, November 27). *New York Times,* Sec. 4, p. 1,2.

32. Ibid.

33. Broder, D. (1983, March 13). There's a gorilla in the hemisphere. *Washington Post,* Sec. B, p. 7.

34. As recalled in Broder's article of 3/13/83.

Chapter 8

Conclusions

NEWS FORM AS "VOICE"

The result of looking beyond quantitative aspects of the news confirms our suspicion that simply counting and categorizing occurrences of voices, story length, and number of Canadian versus American minutes or column inches provides little basis for drawing politically substantive conclusions about the way news mediates international relations. Our earlier research in international news encouraged the conclusion that news voices are not simply human actors. Instead, the form of the news itself is likely to be a contributing political voice in its own right; a political voice that imbues the news with meaning that shapes our understanding of international relations. It appears that the context in which the voices are placed, the political "spin" given them in the midst of news constructions is, after all, the significant factor in understanding the potential for meaning that the news brings to Canadian/American political reality. This is inevitably a matter of form. The challenge lies in describing the potential political significance of news form without falling into the diversion of hyperformalistic analysis in which the obsession with form obfuscates the line of inquiry that helps explain the discursive role of the press in international relations.

TOWARD PUBLIC INTERNATIONALISM: PRESS
INVITATIONS TO INTERNATIONAL POLITICAL DISCOURSE

I have suggested that for politically active people, provocative, challenging, detailed news about international affairs invites a more involving, refined and responsive public discourse about foreign policy in general, and for

141

Canadian/American relations specifically. Because politically active people tend to be more secure in their sense of national identity, they are more likely to reach across international borders and to engage in transnational public discourse that explores alternatives to existing relations. News form is a contributing factor to the relative success or failure of this communication enterprise. For example, media coverage showing a balance of power among nations contributes to a trusting relationship among those nations. Therefore, the ways in which news is cast as public discourse, specifically the nature of the appeals in the news, have profound implications for citizen participation in specific Canadian/American issues. News appeals that inform citizens about international relations in ways that move beyond domestication of world affairs, that evaluate, or perhaps challenge and offer alternatives to existing, constrained relations, that include provocative, even subjective commentary that abandons the hermetic sameness of standard news conventions, and that propose participation in an international forum in which the autonomy of its participants is assured, are likely to invite and encourage transnational public communications.

Although this survey of press examples demonstrates that there exists a rich array of *international* press discourse about the issues reviewed, the American press, through its routine of hyperdomesticating international issues, usually fails to organize this discourse into a dynamic forum of ideas for its news consumers. As we have seen, one individual citizen's response to the cruise issue articulated in the form of a letter to the editor of the *New York Times,* chiding Trudeau for his hypocritical stand on cruise missile tests in light of his U.N. speech stands alone as a detailed citizen's argument displayed in the American press. Meanwhile, journalists, for their part, provided no international context during the period of coverage by revealing challenges to U.S. policy from the international press even though both the Soviet and Canadian press dwelt on a range of challenges to U.S. policies. The success of public transnational communications is largely determined by the extent to which politically active persons from a variety of communications cultures are made aware of shared orientations to specific political issues by the press. For it is here that responses and alternatives to international policy are negotiated.

Four points of invitational coorientation were used to compare the news examples' discursive potential. Each represents the politically active audience confronting news form (i.e., making judgments about the political utility of appeals in the various news types). Figure 8.1 illustrates, in a general and simplified way, the comparative invitational potential of the three primary news types identified in the news examples.[1] The appeals typical of each news source tend to locate it at a particular point along the invitational continuum that is described by the coorientation types. Print commentary is consistently more invitational for each point of coorientation, followed by "hard" news, with television considerably less politically invitational than the print forms.

When the American press, in any of its manifestations (print or television, commentary or "straight" news), accommodates appeals and arguments from foreign presses as part of its reporting about a particular issue, the invitational potential of that news increases for all of the coorientations represented in Fig. 8.1. Public political discourse is better informed and the news consumer's judgmental role as a political player is enhanced. In most cases, the news fails to make such accommodations. The

Invitational —————————— Noninvitational

Disjunction
  Print: Commentary —— News; TV News

  Internationalization
    Print: Commentary —— News; TV News

    Domestication
      Print: Commentary —— News; TV News

      Public Accreditation
        Print: Commentary —— News: TV News

FIG. 8.1. Comparative invitational potential of American news forms at points of coorientation as determined by their predominant appeal.

result is that this news, represents a communications phenomenon that is similar in effect if not intention, to the electronic "jamming" of international broadcast messages. But here we have "jamming" by editorial fiat; by selection, placement and exclusion.

The consequences of such communications decisions are likely to be restricted world views, and an unnecessarily subdued public transnational political discourse. The irony residing in our finding that information routinely classified as propaganda, gathered by American intelligence via FBIS reports is perhaps more useful to internationally tuned citizens than international affairs coverage by the mainstream American press, should not be overlooked. For it points to certain contradictions between the ideal functions of a free press in western democracies as uttered by news professionals, and the cost (to public discourse) of the systematic exclusion of international press opinion as a part of journalists' operational routines.

COMPARATIVE PRESS TREATMENT
OF CANADA'S INTERNATIONAL ROLE

The American press examples reviewed here, in both network television and prestige print press forms, are aggressively ethnocentric, offering the public forum comparatively few opportunities to understand and evaluate specific Canadian/American issues in the context of the larger international community. This news is largely unconnected to and uninformed by international political discourse about Canada's international role. The appeals are framed for a highly generalized, apolitical audience perspective that is locked into a domestic world view. This is a view that neither invites, flatters, nor provides grist for one who brings to the news a knowledge of the historical–political details of Canadian/American relations. And there is little here to encourage the uninformed but curious to learn about Canada. Even the bare essentials about the workings of Canadian domestic politics for the issues covered are absent in the great majority of these news constructions.

World environmental issues are cast in ways that embrace the logic of scientific positivism; environmentally sound alternatives to existing socioeconomic arrangements are rarely mentioned; less frequently encouraged. The American print press seldom recruits Canadians as voices in the news reports. When it does, that representation is part of detailed, subjective commentary. American TV and the Soviet press share the tendency to more frequently include Canadian voices, although the American television coverage strips Canadians out of their domestic and international political arenas and uses them primarily to illustrate American domestic politics. Even in coverage of issues that are essentially Canadian such as the NFB issue, Canada is linked with appeals to tradition that invoke "freedom"; appeals that in the end are concerned about Americans' loss of freedom rather than with the freedom that links the fate of these two countries as correspondents in the larger international community.

Although television news coverage, reflecting the tabloid heritage from which it springs, offers little in the way of inspired, culturally insightful or informative coverage of Canadian affairs, there is a slight difference in news form among American TV networks. ABC, more than the other networks, deviates from standard journalistic conventions in ways that have the potential to provoke political interest and response. But for most audience orientations, these deviations are politically inconsequential. For they are rare, rough gems amidst the total volume of television news that works primarily to deliver audiences through the construction of dramatic episodes. Typically, these episodes are laced together by self-serving, opportunistic journalistic conventions that are characterized by pervasive ethnocentrism. Infrequently, TV news devotes time to a series of reports about an issue by spreading the reports over several broadcasts.

But even in those instances, the networks' myopic rush to construct the "essential" dramatic moment, leads to shifting, contradictory interpretations of the international issue at hand, all the while using the domestic mirror as the primary point of focus. There is little recognition of Canada's distinct politics and culture. Nor are we made aware of the many complex issues contributing to definitions of Canadian/American relations that together define the larger policy context for such issues as acid rain. Beyond a brief glimpse of a Soviet ship in the Halifax harbor in the TV coverage, we are not introduced in any substantive way to the aspirations and activities of Canada as a viable player in the international political community. Trudeau's visit to Russia to meet with Chernenko in February 1984 is reported only in terms of America's political objectives—the likelihood of detente, and speculation about the Soviet leader's health. There was no concern for the larger mission of Trudeau's peace initiative, of the tradition of Canada's international role as peacemaker or of the Canadian domestic political reaction to Trudeau's peace mission. The overriding mythic appeals in the American coverage celebrate Canadian/ U.S. friendship revealing Canada as a follower of U.S. trends and as a country dependent on U.S. military and economic superiority.

Although the NFB coverage comes the closest to representing a Canadian challenge to U.S. power, even that news is preoccupied with the retelling of the myth of American domination. Similarly, the Canadian elections and the free trade issue are put into a "follow America" perspective. The political implications of this form for most audience orientations is convenient for maintaining the status quo of America's Canadian policy. As a result of this overriding mythic focus, there is no forum for a detailed presentation of a Canadian political confrontation with the American way. The dilemma in the end, is not that the American press neglects Canada, as previous quantitative studies would lead us to expect. Rather, the totality of American news treatments, reflecting the arrangements from which their rhetoric springs, provide a vague profile of Canada. That rough sketch presents Canada politically as nothing more than an occasional irritant to certain American objectives. The bulk of the portrayal is based in our economic imperatives; Canada is an important, but culturally faceless marketing opportunity

On the other hand, the international news voices in the non-American FBIS examples provide considerable detail and commentary about Canadian domestic politics, about the presence and political posture of Canada across a range of issues on the world stage, and specifically, about the international implications of Canada's engaging in cruise missile testing with the United States. The Soviet news rests on a haranguing rhetorical foundation of anti-Americanism. And, like the Americans, the Soviets are preoccupied with using Canada as an object around which Soviet/American conflicts can be portrayed in self-serving rhetoric that involves Canada in "dramas of victimage." Images of Canadian sovereignty are invoked by the Soviet press. But the predominant arguments of which they are a part serve the interests of American and Soviet policy. The Soviets use labels and metaphors that invoke images of a shared Soviet/Canadian Northern culture amidst appeals that confront American military policy. These appeals to the Canadian "brotherhood" routinely petition Canadian public opinion as warrants for their claims of shared cultural abuse represented by the American's choice of Canada as a test site because "Canada's geography is similar to the Soviets'." But compared to the American news, the Soviet and other world presses portray Canada as a dynamic, independent actor in international affairs. The Soviet and Chinese press coverage demonstrates that there is world recognition of the considerable cost to Canada's domestic tranquility in Canada's agreeing to the tests. Similarly, Canada's self-proclaimed role of international peacemaker is recognized and played on by the Soviet press. Both of these dimensions and importantly, their saliency for the international community, are ignored in the American press. The world press examples disclose a complex discourse that the American press might have engaged and confronted and in so doing contributed to our understanding of the implications of the cruise test policy and our roles vis-à-vis that policy. The collective failure of the American press to inform us about international reactions to a broad range of North American issues represents a missed communications opportunity of some significance to Canadian/American and Soviet/American relations.

The ways in which the particular issues of acid rain, the NFB controversy cruise missile testing, and free trade were treated by the American press reveal a fractured and unfinished Canadian "image." Separately or in all of its manifestations, the American press fails to offer enough "pieces" to complete its jig-saw construction of Canada. A number of significant pieces are missing. More often than not the American press tends to spotlight relatively insignificant, isolated pieces, forcing them into an American context, leaving them unattached to the larger picture of Canadian/American affairs.

PROPOSITIONS

In order to change the news milieu through which Canadian/American affairs are portrayed, one must recognize the political significance of the distinction between amount and kind of coverage. Diplomatic analysis that evaluates press coverage solely on the basis of minutes of network coverage for Canada rather than the political meanings in that news treatment for politically active constituencies seems misdirected in light of the revelations of this study. News contexts, news consumers' frames of reference and the points of negotiation among them are essential elements in the communication of political power. Unless communication strategists are intent on changing the journalistic formulas that are central to this communication process, more Canadian coverage will become simply more misrepresentation of the distinctiveness and collaborative potential of the Canadian political culture. In order to encourage alternative ways of thinking about the role of the press in international relations, eight propositions based in the perspective of this study are offered here. They represent, in summary fashion, the potential political consequences of the interaction of news language and the political orientations of the news consumer. Although the particular characteristics of the news examples cannot be assumed to be generalizable beyond the context of this study, the propositions might be useful, in a comparative way, to those who study news representations of other countries, or as points for Canadian/American specialists to consider in formulating press strategies.

Proposition 1: Invitational form in international affairs reporting is more closely associated with subjective commentary including informed judgment, disjunctive proposals and international appeals than it is with constructions based in routinized journalistic formulas of objectivity and balance that appeal to domestication and public accreditation.

Therefore, reports about Canadian/American affairs that inform people about international opinion regarding the issue at hand have a greater potential to invite transnational communication than journalism that excludes the international context.

Proposition 2: When television journalists perceive and report conflict rather than consensus among government policymakers, the voices of the news are organized in ways that are more confrontational toward the policy than when government consensus is apparent.[2]

This proposition suggests that an active, adversarial press would, over time, work to Canada's advantage in publicizing alternative policies to existing ones. It also suggests that Canada's current strategy of domesticating its policy with the United States is a sound one to the extent that it fractures consensus among U.S. policymakers about policies that are not in Canada's best interest and, when accommodated by news reports, has the potential to invite the public to participate in the discourse associated with the issue at hand.

Proposition 3: American news stories that directly confront government policy tend to use appeals to an ideal social order rather than appeals to authority.

The implications of this proposition are that when the news speaks with its own voice, as opposed to simply organizing and editing together voices from a range of spokespersons, it tends to use a mode of discourse that appeals to what are perceived as ideal public values, such as the ideal of freedom of speech or international peace. Such appeals encourage rather than constrain transnational communication.

Proposition 4: The greater the intensity, duration, and detail of print and television news confrontations to government policy, the greater the invitation for policy elites to collide in the public media forum.

Implicit in this study are lessons about how news serves up invitations for the American policymaking elite to collide among themselves in order to protect their particular political cultures. For example, as American TV news pressed its confrontation about the National Film Board issue over time, the presumption of increased public pressure and opinion formation among the competing factions of policy elite subcultures encouraged them to respond with public statements designed to protect their own interests and to ascribe the negative elements of the controversial policy to others.

Proposition 5: The news engages scientific discourse in ways that accept and confirm scientific explanations of international political issues.

Typically, news reports of scientific findings are cast as appeals to authority that tend to work against invitations to alternatives to established institutional arrangements and the policies that protect them. Positivism is a preferred meaning in news coverage relating to environmental issues such as acid rain, and in economists' explanations of the impact of free trade. This tendency is most obvious when there is government consensus about the issue in question. If, for example, Congress assumes that the public has accepted the TV news' explanations of acid rain that unquestioningly embrace the latest scientific findings, and are thereby moved to consensus about policy on the basis of that assumption, public discourse about acid rain could be effectively constrained. The re-engagement of the issue in the public forum is left to the domain of interpersonal communication among politically active audience constituencies and their selective use of alternative media channels.

Proposition 6: Canadian/American issues of significant interest to warrant more than a single day's television coverage receive increasingly similar treatment across networks in terms of appeals used and the political interpretations that are rendered.

One explanation for this phenomenon is that the formal and informal channels among journalists and media managers move toward consensus in the manner of "pack journalism" and the productions coalesce in style and content. This tendency reveals the need for studying informal and professional, off-screen communications in order to fully understand the policy implications of news processes. This proposition suggests that the Canadians might benefit from more aggressively infusing the American news system with news releases that include details of Canada's position on particular political issues, and insights into the elements of Canadian culture.

Proposition 7: American print and television news representations of Canada favor issues that are American-centered and these issues are interpreted in ways that work against the image of Canada as an independent international entity.

This kind of news treatment tends to use Canadian/American relations more for purposes of enhancing the rhetorical authority of the news than to propose or legitimate Canadian/American collaborations per se. Past quantitative research has demonstrated that a greater volume of U.S. news coverage is routinely given to nations that are assumed to be in a confrontational or strategic relationship with the United States. Alternately, the proposition offered here suggests that *qualitatively* the meaning of foreign affairs news aggressively favors American political interests even when friendly nations are the subjects of the news coverage. As a result of this preoccupation, very little is revealed about the details of Canadian politics and culture in general. News coverage of the free trade issue is an obvious example of this tendency.

Proposition 8: Television news, compared to print news, is more sensitive to elements that contribute to dramatic tension than to elements that inform discourse about the details of policy.

The priority of the news is to construct dramatic tension first, then superficially attend to the policy issue around which the drama is framed.

However, dramatic constructions are not inherently more or less significant to policy that guides Canadian American relations than those constructions associated with the McNeil–Leher "talking-head" public broadcasting format. The orientation of the news consumer, in large part, determines the political consequences of such constructions. However, in the long run, the negative effect of the TV news networks' tendency to select events that facilitate dramatic treatment might be to define Canadian/American relations extremely narrowly rather than to reveal the many points of mutual interest and potential collaboration that in fact are a part of our interactions.

Together, the propositions suggest that the model of democratic pluralism, an orientation frequently used by students of international relations, is a simplified view of news mediation of policy. It is a perspective that is likely to overstate the power of individual news reports on public opinion, to underestimate the intricacies of media form as they relate to the language of politics, and to overlook the complexity with which media audiences attend to and use media.

NOTES

1. Because a person could conceivably negotiate several news coorientations at the same time, it is likely that responses to the news forms represented here are considerably more complex than this linear configuration suggests.

2. This proposition recalls a similar cause–effect relationship suggested by Paletz and Entman: "When public officials are in disagreement over a foreign policy issue, mass media coverage may present a wider range of information and alternatives for public consumption" (p. 231). Paletz, D., Entman, R. Op. Cit.

Author Index

Subject Index